SPEAKING
FOR
SUCCESS

Readings and Resources

Second Edition

Edited by

Steven D. Cohen

Jeanette Henderson and Roy Henderson

Preface

Speaking for Success: Readings and Resources is designed to help students master the art and practice of public speaking. Like my courses at Harvard, this collection challenges students to identify their own public speaking behaviors and change the way they prepare for presentations. It builds upon and extends the ideas in *Public Speaking: The Path to Success*—an action-oriented guide that teaches students how to speak with confidence and leave a lasting impression. Together, these two books provide students with the knowledge they need to change hearts and change minds every time they speak.

This collection explores the tools and techniques that powerful speakers use to captivate their listeners. Unlike traditional academic readers, this collection of readings and resources maintains a strong focus on praxis. To that end, I have shied away from articles that merely discuss public speaking theory. Instead, I have selected articles that help students understand what to do and how to do it. I also have included articles that focus on first impressions, leadership styles, and public narratives. In many ways, these articles are just as important—if not more so—than the articles on specific techniques. After all, powerful public speaking is not simply about delivering an effective message; it is also about demonstrating one's capacity and readiness to lead.

Speaking for Success: Readings and Resources is divided into three main parts. The first part, "Developing a Leadership Mindset," explores the relationship between leadership and public speaking. Given that a speaker's job is to lead the audience toward a particular objective, it is important that students think about themselves as speakers and as leaders. Once students develop the appropriate mindset, they will be able to focus on the message itself. The second part, "Crafting Memorable Messages," introduces students to the attributes of well-designed presentations. Students will learn how to transform their ideas into a compelling presentation that engages the audience and strikes the right tone. After developing the presentation, students will need help refining their delivery. The third part, "Delivering Powerful Presentations," examines the interplay between speakers and listeners. It equips students to stand in front of a room and make an impact—on their audience and on the world around them.

Over the years, I have worked with many students who were afraid of speaking in class or in the workplace. These students wondered whether they ever would be able to stand up and speak up about something that mattered to them. With practice and persistence, however, these students were able to show others (and frankly, show themselves) that they had what it took to succeed. My hope is that other students will use the frameworks and strategies in this book to conquer their own public speaking challenges—for if they do, they soon will find themselves on the path to success.

— *Steven D. Cohen*

Part I

Developing a Leadership Mindset

A View from the Balcony

By Steven D. Cohen

Step back and see how your audience is observing you.

Every time you deliver a speech, you are, in fact, leading. Whether you are a student, an executive, a politician or a professor, you must lead your audience toward a particular objective. Your job isn't simply to communicate ideas to your audience members—it is to show them you are a leader.

As part of this process, you must think about how your audience members perceive you when you are standing in front of the room. You must examine what you do well and how you can improve. But how do you achieve this perspective?

In *Leadership on the Line: Staying Alive Through the Dangers of Leading*, Ronald A. Heifetz and Martin Linsky talk about the importance of "getting off the dance floor and going to the balcony." It's a metaphor that emphasizes the need for leaders to step back in the middle of a situation and ask themselves, What's really going on here? The "balcony" is a place where you can see yourself clearly and observe how your audience members respond to you.

Assessing Your Performance

You can reach the balcony in many different ways. For example, you might pause for a moment after sharing an important idea and mentally observe your audience members' reactions. Or, you might ask a couple of colleagues to watch you deliver a speech and share their observations with you. You can even videotape yourself and review your speech at a later time. Whatever strategy you choose, you'll gain insight into how to improve your performance.

Stepping onto the balcony allows you to focus on what is actually happening rather than on what you are saying. From the balcony, you can feel the emotion and capture the energy in the room. Once you more firmly understand what your audience members experience while you are speaking, you will know exactly what actions to take.

That's the key—taking action. Thinking and analyzing are the easy parts; the hard part is changing your behavior the *next time* you speak. Indeed, powerful public speaking, much like leadership, requires that you constantly assess and improve your performance.

When I was in college, I remember hearing all sorts of filler words pop out of my mouth. It wasn't until I attended my first Toastmasters meeting that I realized I had a problem. When the Ah-Counter listed the total number of filler words I had used, I asked myself: Did I really say "um" that many times? The Ah-Counter, in a sense, helped me get on the balcony and understand what my audience was hearing. Armed with this knowledge, I knew exactly what to do: Pause more frequently to reduce my use of filler words.

Identifying Your Default Speaking Settings

Each of us has default settings—automatic, pre-programmed behaviors that are comfortable and familiar. For example, when someone sneezes, we typically say "Bless you." We don't stop to think about why we say it—we just say it. We also have default ways of getting dressed in the morning, preparing certain meals and walking from one place to another.

Similarly, we each have default public speaking settings—ingrained ways of communicating and interacting with our audience members. However, some of these default settings may actually impede our ability to make a powerful impact on our listeners.

To become a powerful public speaker, you must identify your ingrained speaking patterns and determine the impact that they are having on your capacity to lead. Do you nervously adjust your glasses or run your hands through your hair? Do you say "um" or "uh" every few words? Once you identify these habits, you can challenge yourself to adjust them.

Making Positive Changes

It is important to remember that making significant adjustments isn't an easy process. It may take time and the changes may feel uncomfortable for awhile, but the results are typically well worth the effort.

I often push my University of Maryland and Harvard Extension School students to adjust their default settings in real time. At the beginning of every semester, I ask the students to stand in the center of the speaking area and introduce themselves to the class. Some students really struggle with this exercise and default to sharing impersonal, bland introductions. Here is an example:

> *My name is Susan. I've been in school for a couple years now, but I'm nearing the end of the road. I come from a large family in central New York and found my way here after living in a bunch of places. So, yeah. That's about it.*

It's not that students like Susan don't have anything interesting to say; they just don't know *what* to say. I help them *get on the balcony* by suggesting that they ask their peers for feedback. When they do that, the students discover they had sounded rather uninspired. I encourage them to share their passions with their listeners. When the students begin again, they instantly become more animated.

Like Susan, you must push yourself to adjust. The perfect place to do that is in Toastmasters. But you can't expect to become a powerful public speaker after attending a few club meetings. You need time to change the habits that are holding you back.

In his 2008 book *Outliers: The Story of Success,* Malcolm Gladwell discusses the fundamental importance of practice. What "distinguishes one performer from another is how hard he or she works," writes Gladwell. "That's it. And what's more, the people at the very top don't just work harder ... than everyone else. They work much, *much* harder."

The only way to "reprogram" your speaking patterns is to embrace the art of practice. Make public speaking a hobby by seeking opportunities to speak. Ask to introduce a keynote speaker. Volunteer to speak at a company function. Fill a Toastmasters club meeting role. It doesn't matter where you speak. What matters is that you push yourself to get on the balcony over and over again.

If you commit to examining and adjusting your default public speaking settings, you will dramatically enhance your ability to lead.

Just What is Leadership?

By Tim Tobin

In this chapter, I want to help you understand what I call *the ecology of leadership*. Obviously, someone cannot be much of a leader if no one is there to be led. So it's a delicate environment of projects, priorities, and plans as well as emotions, sensitivities, and ambitions.

President Eisenhower once commented, "Leadership is the art of getting someone to do something you want done because he wants to do it." Ike's approach to delegation could be called subtle. But to him, delegation was an important skill and a big deal. It surely served him well in Europe as he dealt with many big egos to lead the Allied effort in World War II.

A Word About Perceptions

Speaking of Ike, we typically don't think of him as having had a big ego. Supreme Allied commander, president of Columbia University, general of the Army, president of the United States. That's a résumé that would enable anyone's ego to balloon. But not Eisenhower. He was awesome and not awesome at the same time.

Likewise, it is important for all of us to understand how we are perceived by others and where that is consistent with our self-perceptions. If there is misalignment between the two, it is important to understand why that is. As the introduction implies, this [chapter's] process and steps are not intended to reaffirm to you that you are just so awesome right now. In a few paragraphs, you will meet Bob and watch his lunch mates tell him how not awesome he really is. It is a shocker for him.

What is Your Leadership Story?

The truth is, you are only as good a leader as people think you are. That's hard to accept if you wear awesomeness on your sleeve. A self-review of your leadership would contain inherent flaws, and too often leaders attempt to rationalize their behavior. According to the book *Leadership and Self-Deception*, by the Arbinger Institute, leaders can blind themselves to their true motivations and capabilities. Without a review from others, it is unlikely that our self-perception is accurate—whether positive or critical. Rarely is our own perception exactly right. And that has implications for our ability to lead others effectively.

Our awareness and acceptance of our imperfections is the pathway to excellence. To that end, this [chapter] establishes a system of checks and balances to help you to truly understand who you are as a leader, based not only on your perceptions but also on the perceptions and interpretations of others. You may not like what you hear. It may not align with your self-image. But it is critical to fully understanding your story. Think of it this way: The value added is balance.

Your leadership story is the intersection between what you believe your story to be and others' interpretations. It is reflected in what you say and do as well as how others perceive and interpret what you say and do as a leader. And to add to the complexity, others' interpretations may not be accurate. Or worse, their motivations may not support your story.

This paradox of who owns your story is a constant struggle. Are you the primary author? Or does your story live in the interpretations of others? The answer is yes to both. If you do not take primary author-ship of your story, it will be crafted exclusively through the perceptions of others. That will not be a very accurate autobiography. The following figure illustrates the importance of understanding and aligning your leadership story with the perceptions of others. It also shows the prob-lems of being misunderstood.

Your leadership story currently exists somewhere within the quad-rants above. Each is described in detail below. Your story can manifest itself positively or negatively in each of the quadrants. Your objective is to understand your leadership story, work to get it to where you want it to be, and make sure that others are aligned with it.

Figure 2-1 Variations (or Interpretations) of Your Leadership Story

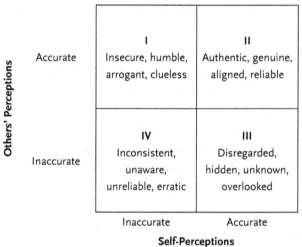

Quadrant 1

This is a difficult place for leaders to find themselves in. It suggests that others know you better than you know yourself. On a slightly positive note, leaders here do not believe in themselves, nor do they believe that they have great attributes as a leader, and this may show itself as being humble. But even humility has a dark side: over time, others will eventually not believe in you, either.

Jeff lived in Q1. Everyone thought he was great, but he was quick to deflect praise. He would always say, "No, no. I didn't do that. My team did." Noble indeed. People appreciated his humility, but eventually he convinced others that he really couldn't do it, and that fate became part of his story. In a sense, he wrote it himself.

Ben was a leader who ran into this challenge. He was viewed by many as humble. He did not take credit for his expertise and leadership capabilities. When others gave him credit, he was quick to deflect it and say, "Oh, I'm not sure I did that." He was admired by many, and then, over time, others began to question his abilities. It began simply enough, with a few peers and leaders saying, "I'm not sure," about his abilities. Although his story never left Quadrant I, it quickly transitioned from humility to a question of capability. He had effectively talked others into not believing in him. An adage comes to mind: If you believe you can't do something, you are probably right.

Another type exists in this quadrant. They are the leaders who are narcissistic, self-important, or overconfident. Leaders here think they are awesome—and they aren't afraid to let others know it through their words or actions. However, awesome is not how they are perceived by others. In either case, these leaders either are clueless or simply don't care how they are showing up as a leader. Your solution, if you find yourself to be in this quadrant, is to seek feedback and listen to others. You may find it beneficial to do a skills audit and to work on your executive presence.

Quadrant 2

Using the story as a metaphor, this quadrant is known as a leader's true story. Leaders in this quadrant have a good understanding of their leadership story, and others do as well. Leaders here are viewed as authentic—what you see is what you get. They are genuine. They know their strengths and areas for development, and they tend to be willing to enlist the support of others.

Even if these leaders' stories have negative attributes, they are aware of this and either take corrective action individually or are conscious of when and how to supplement their skills. But leaders here should not get too comfortable. If you find yourself in this space, you should continue to reflect, be self-aware, and enlist others to tell their story.

Randy may not have had all the answers, but he was willing to bring in others to help. He had great ideas, but he knew he wasn't an expert in everything. His go-to phrase was "What do you think?" You felt like you knew him on a personal level and that he cared about you. And he was passionate about the work he was doing.

Quadrant 3

Leaders here are, well, hidden. They have a good understanding of their story, but no one else does. Because others don't know who these leaders are, they tend to be overlooked.

If you know your story and it is negative, you may lack credibility and will have some work to do to become a better leader. If you know who you are as a leader and it is positive, you need to become better known as a leader. If you are in this quadrant, focus on building your network, get involved throughout the organization in projects and initiatives, and enlist others to tell your leadership story.

Jeremy was a leader who fit this description. He was new to the organization, fresh out of graduate school. He had a lot of bright ideas but no way of sharing them. It wasn't his style to aggressively assert himself, and he didn't want to come across as bragging or trying to take charge. But eventually he became frustrated. He and I worked on ways to build his internal network and get involved in projects to showcase what he was capable of.

Quadrant 4

These leaders are inconsistent and unclear at best; they are erratic and unreliable at worst. Just as in Quadrant I, such leaders lack self-awareness. They lack thought and reflection about who they are as leaders, what they value, and what they stand for.

Many leaders here have not taken the time to understand who they are or what they believe in as a leader. To make this quadrant more directly personal to you, no one else knows you or what you believe in, either. People may follow you because you are the boss, but they are skeptical and reluctant to do so.

If you find yourself in this quadrant, you should begin by understanding your leadership story. As a starting point, focus on what you believe in and value as a leader. The good news is that almost any action you take toward understanding, aligning, or communicating your leadership story is a step in the right direction.

Sam was an established leader within the organization, due in large part to his technical knowledge. Sometimes he wanted to get into the details and sometimes he didn't. He would assign tasks and follow up on some but not others. None of Sam's direct reports knew what to expect from him, nor did some of his peers. How do you think his team felt? He never thought about how this was affecting his team—creating low morale, poor performance, and a sense of uncertainty. Others viewed him as volatile and inconsistent.

Types of Leadership

What type of leadership do you want to master? What leadership style do you aspire to? You need to think about what type of leader you want to be. And here is the fun part about leadership: there is not one single best way to lead.

The choice is yours. Choose the kind of leadership, or combination thereof, that best suits you and that you aspire to. The purpose of this activity is not merely to increase self-awareness. It will help you to consider the ultimate goals of leadership so that you keep in mind the importance of your leadership for the greater good. The result will be a more meaningful goal—or set of goals—that brings fulfillment to you and those you lead.

There are many types of leadership. What does leadership mean to you? What is the role and purpose of a leader? As you think about your own definition of leadership, some of the words you used may have given you a clue as to what style of leadership you gravitate toward. Did you use words such as *help* or *serve others*? Did you talk about developing others? Do you look at leadership as a process? Is it interactive? With whom? As you think about the kind of leader you want to be, consider the various types of leadership described in the table below.

Figure 2-2   Types of Leadership

Type of Leadership	Illustrative Perspectives
Servant leadership	Robert Greenleaf, Ken Blanchard, Mark Miller
Purpose-driven leadership	Bill George, Clayton Christensen
Positive leadership	Robert Quinn, Ryan Quinn, Kim Cameron
Appreciative Inquiry leadership	David Cooperrider, Diana Whitney, Ed Schein
Stewardship leadership	Peter Block, Nelson Mandela
Conversations That Matter leadership	Meg Wheatley, Bev Kaye, Sharon Jordan-Evans, Juanita Brown
Peer-to-peer leadership	Mila Baker, Bill George
Benevolent dictatorship	So many examples
Command-and-control leadership	Some very famous examples

Toward a Balanced Leadership Story for You

This [chapter] is about getting your leadership story straight. It is about facing the realities of your leadership story from multiple angles. It is about understanding who you are as a leader and who you want to be.

It is also about understanding and aligning your beliefs as a leader with the perceptions of others—that critical balance. In short, [it] is about understanding, aligning, and communicating who you are as a leader.

Two Big Questions

[This chapter] concerns two important questions, so let's try to answer them.

What Makes Great Leadership?

Many definitions of leadership exist—too many to mention here. What does great leadership mean to you? And what does it mean in the context of your organization?

Look around you at the various leaders you deal with regularly. What do they do that is inspiring? Uninspiring? There are plenty of examples of great leaders and bad leaders. Wherever you stand on the spectrum of great-to-poor leaders and whatever your definition of leadership is, I would have one question for you: How is that working for you? If everything is going perfectly, keep up the good work. For most leaders, there are opportunities for improvement somewhere in their skill set.

Despite the complexity of leadership, there seem to be some common attributes, skills, and characteristics among great leaders. Leaders have to be technically competent. But technical competence can be both a hindrance and a requirement to be a great leader.

I refer to technical competence as a critical part of your leadership foundation because you have to have technical competence and understand the business you are in before you can be a leader. At the same time, as you take on leadership responsibilities, you will have to let go of some of your technical responsibilities—that which got you here—in order to embrace leadership. You need to take time to understand the various aspects of the business you are in, the competitive landscape, and the operating environment in order to make good, fundamentally sound, and relevant business decisions.

Technical competence can be a barrier to great leadership for two reasons. First, being technically competent does not automatically ensure leadership competence. I have seen this firsthand on numerous occasions where a perfectly capable employee gets promoted into a leadership position and fails as a leader. Second, leaders with technical expertise may have a difficult time letting go of their technical responsibilities. I have seen leaders continue to spend time on aspects of their job that they should delegate. Great leaders need to focus on leadership.

Great leadership requires providing vision and direction. It requires motivating and inspiring people to work toward the vision. It requires developing other people. And it requires achieving results. In short, leadership is about people. Your ability to connect with people can make all the difference between great and poor leadership. Where this gets particularly complex is that different people have different needs, and those needs may shift over time, along with a host of other changing variables. Leadership is a dynamic, moving target that requires you to be thoughtful and prepared in your approach. Your leadership story serves as an anchor and foundation for your actions as a leader.

Great leaders have a plan, and also they are great improvisers. Just as a good actor has to improvise onstage if something unplanned happens, great business leaders, as improvisers, are the actor, writer, and director of their story. They must act in the moment. As writer, they must initiate ideas. And as director, they must provide a bigger view and facilitate room for ideas, creativity, and action.

Why Focus on Your Leadership Story?

You are the actor, writer, and director of your leadership story. You act in the moment, initiate ideas, provide a bigger view, and allow for ideas and creativity. Understanding and communicating your leadership story can be quite powerful. It provides clarity around what you stand for as a leader. It keeps alive the people, values, and life lessons that you hold dear. It gives you the power of influence and authenticity by allowing you to match your words and your actions. It allows you to build trust. Trust leads to credibility.

By helping you to understand what has shaped you as a leader, your leadership story can make the strong emotional connection that is necessary to inspire and motivate others. It can also be a useful tool with which to impart knowledge and lessons to others— to help them learn from the experiences that have shaped your leadership story. And it provides you and others with insights into what you hold important as a leader.

By understanding your leadership story, you will have greater self-awareness and fewer blind spots. It will also provide a starting point for you as you continue to develop as a leader. It will guide you in modifying your story so that you can be a better leader. When you effectively communicate your leadership story, you and others will have clarity about your expectations as a leader.

Leadership is a journey that involves the past, the present, and the future. Once upon a time, your leadership story was a blank page filled with hopes, dreams, opportunities, and inspiration. For many, those hopes and dreams included being a great leader. As you have realized some hopes and dreams, and have learned more through experience about what makes a great leader, perhaps new or revised ideas around being a great leader have sprung up.

What has contributed to the evolution of your notions about leadership? What has supported you in your personal quest to be a great leader? What has inhibited you from being your best? Looking ahead, what are you prepared to do to be the best leader you can be?

My six-year-old daughter recently told me something profound and relevant to understanding our leadership story. She said, "First you plant a seed. Then you nourish it. Then it sprouts. Then it grows. Finally, it turns into a flower."

Our nourishment for growth and development consists of reflection, action, and insights. Let's face it—we operate in a very action-oriented environment. We spend more time on action and results that reward us, and far less time on thinking and reflecting. Reflection is a process of understanding what happened and why. It creates self-awareness. A lack of self-awareness leads to blind spots, and at the least it puts you at a disadvantage as a leader.

Who's got time for this reflection and self-awareness? I would re-state that: Who has time to get leadership wrong? When you combine self-awareness with a willingness to stretch outside your comfort zone, you will see the greatest breakthroughs and maximize your leadership potential.

Learning plays a key role in developing your story. Reflection is about asking yourself questions. It may require thinking differently and taking action in order to build capability. Once you have mastered your leadership story, you will make stronger connections and inspire, energize, and motivate those you lead. You will be a better leader.

When I run workshops for leaders, at the end of the session, I ask the group a simple question: "So what?" So what did you learn from this? And so what are you going to do with it? I ask for only a few of the key concepts they learned, as I have found that to be more realistic in initiating change. If you gain insights without action, this book will be only partially useful. However, if you gain insights *and* take action, this book will be much more useful and potentially transformational. When you finish this book, ask yourself the same questions: What did I learn—about myself, about leadership, and about my leadership story? And what am I willing and prepared to do about it?

References

The Arbinger Institute. (2010). *Leadership and self-deception: Getting out of the box.* San Francisco, CA: Berrett-Koehler Publishers.

Psych Yourself Up, Not Out

By Sam Horn

I get nervous if I don't get nervous. I think it's healthy. You
just have to channel that into the show.

~ **Singer Beyoncé**

An entrepreneur asked me, almost in a state of panic, "My laptop froze in the middle of a crucial presentation last week. It took me forever to get my slides working again, but by then it was too late. I'd lost everyone's attention and couldn't get them back. I've got another presentation coming up and I'm afraid of another meltdown. Can you help me regain my confidence?"

I asked her, "Are you an athlete?"

"Yes, but what does that have to do with regaining my confidence?"

"Because you've played sports, you know there are two kinds of athletes when the game's on the line. The kind who step back and say, 'DON'T give me the ball.' And the kind who step up and say, 'Give me the ball.'" I looked her straight in the eye and said, "I bet you're the latter."

She laughed and said, "You're right."

"That's why, from now on, you're going to see speaking as a sport so you can walk in and project a 'Gimme the ball' kind of confidence that helps you feel, look, and act like a winner."

Tennis champ Chris Evert was asked, on the first day of the tournament, if Serena Williams had a chance of winning the 2014 US Open. Chris said, "We all know confidence is the name of the game for her." Confidence is the name of the game for *all* of us. Fortunately, it is a learnable skill, not a mysterious ability we either have or don't. These four steps can help you channel nervousness into the "show," so you can walk into any interaction, raring to go.

See Communication as a Sport

She walks out like she expects to win. She looks like she belongs.
~ Patrick McEnroe, talking about fifteen-year-old tennis player CiCi Bellis at the 2014 US Open

Here are the steps I shared with my client to help her psych herself up instead of out. Remember: you act in accordance with your expectations. Prepare for high-stakes communications just like you would a championship match. These steps can help you walk in expecting to command attention and respect and feeling and looking like you belong. This is not trivial. After all, how can people have confidence in you if you don't have confidence in yourself?

1. Go for a walk/rehearse.

Have you been told to practice what you want to say in front of a mirror? That's terrible advice! That focuses you on *you*, which makes you overly self-aware. It's smarter to get out of your head and get moving so you practice multifocus concentration.

What's multifocus concentration? It is that stream-of-conscious (versus self-conscious) flow in which athletes are able to stay focused while adapting to changing circumstances.

Think about it. Baseball players have to anticipate what pitch is coming, plan how to hit it while glancing to see if their teammate is stealing second base. Soccer players pass the ball to a running teammate while avoiding a defender and checking where the goalie is positioned.

How do you, as a communicator, get good at this multifocus concentration that pro athletes have mastered? You get out from behind that desk and get moving. A 2014 Stanford study found that "walking improves creative output by an average of 60 percent."

When you walk/rehearse, you pay attention to the skateboarder and cyclist coming your way while crafting what you want to say. You're, literally and figuratively, getting good at thinking on your feet. You are envisioning how to get and keep your decision-makers' eyebrows up while adapting to your surroundings. That is the multifocus concentration state you want to be in when delivering that presentation, interviewing for that job, or negotiating that contract.

2. Have a flexible game plan.

Never, ever memorize a script or rely on reading from a teleprompter. That disconnects you from the group because it locks your attention on your notes or the screen. Why should your audience pay attention to *you* if you're not paying attention to *them*? Plus, if one thing goes wrong, you're lost because you're in your head instead of in the moment.

Communication is not about delivering prepared remarks verbatim. Intriguing communication is about connecting with people so you see the light go on in their eyes. It involves monitoring your group to see whether they're engaged, apathetic, clear, or confused—and adapting what you say, in real time, based on their expressions.

3. Give yourself home-field advantage.

Why do most sports teams have better records at home than they do away? Because we feel safe in familiar surroundings and can relax and give full attention to our performance.

That's not the case on the road. We are wired for "fight or flight" in new surroundings. We're distracted as we're monitoring our unfamiliar surroundings to see if we're in danger or at risk.

That's why it's in your best interest to familiarize yourself with the location of your interaction before the "real thing." For example, when I'm keynoting a conference, I always check out the hotel ballroom when no one's around (even if that's the previous night). I take the stage, throw my voice to the back of the room, and practice my opening at full volume.

Why is that important? Football coach Pop Warner said, "You play the way you practice." You can't practice at 50 percent and expect to be 100 percent in the real thing. Practicing the *way* you want to play, *where* you're going to play, means you've "been there, done that" so you can focus and give your full attention to connecting with your audience instead of feeling uncomfortable.

4. Tower, don't cower.

If you look meek and weak, you'll feel meek and weak. That's a problem because decision-makers don't respect people who don't command respect.

Unfortunately, that's what happened to a speaker who lost her audience at hello. The opening program started with Jim Collins (*Good to Great*) and then segued into Tom Peters (*In Search of Excellence*) and Seth Godin (*Linchpin*). We were all on the edge of our seats.

The next keynoter took center stage (good for her for getting out from behind the lectern), but then stood with her feet together, her head tucked down, and her hands in the dreaded fig leaf position. She said in a sing-songy voice, "I was telling my granddaughters yesterday how much I was looking forward to this..."

Within seconds, the digital devices came out and people started walking out. Which was a shame because, once she got going, she had valuable insights to share about her company's role in helping victims of 9/11. Unfortunately, her "cower" posture led people to conclude she wasn't worth listening to, and they didn't stay around to hear her program.

If you want to capture and keep people's attention, it's important to project a leadership presence that says, "I know what I'm talking about. You can trust me to add value." You can do that by adopting the "I'm ready for anything" posture athletes assume when playing their sport. You can probably picture it. They have their:

- Feet shoulder-width apart so they're balanced and grounded
- Knees slightly bent so they're flexible and can move easily in any direction
- Head and chin up and eyes focused forward
- Hands centered in front, about a foot apart, like they're holding a basketball

Try it right now. Stand up, put your feet shoulder-width apart, bend your knees, pick your chin up, have basketball hands. That's the tower posture. Now, adopt the cower posture of the speaker who lost her audience. Put your:

- Feet close together. Do you feel unbalanced, "tipsy," like you're a pushover?
- Knees locked tight. Do you feel rigid, uptight, inflexible?
- Head down. Do you feel shy, coy, disconnected from your audience?
- Hands in the fig leaf position. Do you feel awkward, like you have something to hide?

Feel the difference? Choosing to tower, instead of cower, can help you command attention and respect. And in case you're wondering, yes, you can tower while sitting in an interview, meeting, or business meal. Just lift those shoulders, roll them back, and sit tall instead of slouching or slumping. There, doesn't that feel better? You will feel and look more confident and command more confidence from decision-makers when you choose to tower instead of cower.

Create Your Own Confidence Ritual

When you play under pressure every day, your rituals keep you
100 percent focused on what you're doing.
~ Wimbledon champion tennis player Rafael Nadal

I'll always be grateful to two-time Grand Slam tennis champ "Rocket" Rod Laver for teaching me the importance of psyching myself *up* versus *out* with a personalized confidence ritual.

I had the privilege of comanaging Rod's tennis facility on Hilton Head Island in South Carolina. One day, he was gracious enough to ask if I wanted to hit some balls. Unfortunately, I was distracted with some logistics for a national tennis camp we were hosting the following week, and I was spraying balls all over the place. It was embarrassing. I finally said, "Rocket, I appreciate you rallying with me, but I'm wasting your time. We might as well quit."

Rocket looked at me and said, "The mark of a pro is the ability to turn around a bad day."

"But how do you do that?"

"You figure out the key part of your game and figure out a ritual around it. If the key to your game is getting your first serve in, you repeat 'first serve in' and give that all your attention. It gives you something to focus on instead of mentally being all over the map."

Rocket was right about the power of rituals. Does the name Pavlov ring a bell? Rituals are the secret to automatically focusing your attention on what you *do* want versus what you *don't* want.

Your goal is to create a confidence ritual you do religiously before every high-stakes communication. If you're a speaker, it may be saying, "I'm here to serve, not to shine; to make a difference, not to make a name" so you focus on what matters, which is connecting with and adding value to your audience. If you're interviewing for a job, it could be saying, "I'm going to find out and focus on what *their* needs are and how I can contribute to their organization" instead of "I've been out of work for ten months. *I need this job.*"

Figure 4-5 Cuddy and her Princeton adviser, Professor Susan Fiske, on Commencement Day in 2005, when she received her Ph.D.

Courtesy Susan Fiske

another person, she says; rather, it helps you operate at your best. As she explains in her TED talk, "Don't leave that situation feeling like, 'Oh, I didn't show them who I am.' Leave that situation feeling like, 'Oh, I really feel like I got to say who I am and show who I am.'"

Outside of her classes at Harvard, where Cuddy arrived in 2008 after teaching at Rutgers and Northwestern, she gives speeches about her work to groups ranging from management consultants at Accenture to Canadian trial lawyers to editors at Cosmopolitan. She uses catchy images and clear language, shares her bright smile, and has a strong stage presence, a legacy of her ballet training. She also doesn't take herself too seriously, ending one presentation by playing the Wonder Woman theme song and, during another, clasping a pencil between her teeth to demonstrate that forcing yourself to smile can elevate your mood. "She has a sense of style about how she presents ideas," says her mentor, Fiske. Her talks "are straight to the point and aesthetically appealing." She also is working on a book about how people can "nudge" themselves psychologically to improve their confidence, performance, and general well-being.

Cuddy says she has received about 10,000 emails from people living all over the world who use power poses. Among them: people recovering from brain injuries, professional athletes, adults and children in an anti-bullying group, horse trainers, and performing artists. One man wrote to tell her that his boss, a member of Congress, calls the power poses "doing his Supermans." Harvard's assistant volleyball coach, Jeffrey Aucoin, plans to use power posing to help his players "come out onto the court and act like they own the place."

For Sarita Gupta, who often gives speeches on workers' rights as executive director of Jobs With Justice, power poses "help me feel I'm in control of the moment. As a woman of color and a younger woman, how do I show up with authority?" Before addressing a crowd of thousands at a convention recently, she ducked behind a black screen that was onstage to "get big," as she calls it. "I don't care if I look really ridiculous. It reminds me I want to be powerful."

Cuddy's findings have spawned spinoff research: Two professors have found that people who adopted a power pose displayed higher pain thresholds. The study "suggests that power posing may be a useful tool for pain management. Even individuals who do not perceive themselves as having control over their circumstances may benefit from behaving as if they do by adopting power poses," the researchers wrote. Cuddy, meanwhile, is studying the outcomes of negotiations when power posing is done beforehand, and whether the poses can improve physical coordination. She and a colleague are examining whether power posing affects financial decision-making by poor people in Kenya. And she is working with computer scientists to develop a game that incorporates power posing with the aim of reducing children's math anxiety.

The ease of doing power poses—and the accessibility of Cuddy's TED talk explaining them—has enabled her work to spread far beyond her Harvard lab, which makes her very happy. "What matters the most to me is sharing the science," Cuddy says. She likes using that science to "find small tweaks to improve our own outcomes and well-being," she says. "I like figuring out how we can help ourselves be better."

Public Speaking

By Arthur Asa Berger

1. **Know your material.** Pick a topic you are interested in. Know more about it than you include in your speech. Use humor, personal stories and conversational language— that way you won't easily forget what to say.
2. **Practice. Practice. Practice!** Rehearse out loud with all equipment you plan on using. Revise as necessary. Work to control filler words. Practice, pause and breathe. Practice with a timer and allow time for the unexpected.
3. **Know the audience.** Greet some of the audience members as they arrive. It's easier to speak to a group of friends than to strangers.
4. **Know the room.** Arrive early, walk around the speaking area and practice using the microphone and any visual aids.
5. **Relax.** Begin by addressing the audience. It buys you time and calms your nerves. Pause, smile and count to three before saying anything. ("One one-thousand, two one-thousand, three one-thousand. Pause. Begin.) Transform nervous energy into enthusiasm.
6. **Visualize yourself giving your speech.** Imagine yourself speaking, your voice loud, clear and confident. Visualize the audience clapping —it will boost your confidence.

Arthur Asa Berger, "Public Speaking," Messages: An Introduction to Communication, pp. 199-215. Copyright © 2015 by Taylor & Francis Group. Reprinted with permission.

7. **Realize that people want you to succeed.** Audiences want you to be interesting, stimulating, informative and entertaining. They're rooting for you.

8. **Don't apologize** for any nervousness or problem—the audience probably never noticed it.

9. **Concentrate on the message—not the medium.** Focus your attention away from your own anxieties and concentrate on your message and your audience.

Toastmasters International, an organization devoted to helping people become good public speakers—whose advice on public speaking is cited above—was founded to solve the problem that speaking in public is said to be one of the most anxiety-producing activities for most people. That is because they fear they will bore others, that they have nothing interesting to say, and that people to whom they are speaking may show signs of displeasure, heckle them, or even get up and walk out of the room where they are speaking. These acts humiliate us and attack our sense of self, but this kind of behavior is very rare. After learning a few essential tricks of the trade and practicing a bit, most people can do a decent job of public speaking. One secret is to be yourself and draw upon your own sense of humor and your style of doing things.

Public Speaking as a Performance

It is useful to think of public speaking as a kind of performance and you as an actor or actress who has to keep the attention of your audience for an hour—or whatever period of time you have with them. Audiences are fickle, so you must find a way to catch their attention and hold it, just the way actors do in plays. And what do you have to do this? Your presence (your body language, your facial expression, the clothes you are wearing), your personality, your use of language or "voice," your style, and your knowledge. Really great speakers can hold an audience's attention for a long time without using PowerPoint or other audio-visual aids. And that's because an audience feels that what the speaker has to say is important and useful.

We will understand public speaking to involve a person speaking directly to an audience that ranges from a relatively small number of people at a club meeting or a classroom to a large member of people in an auditorium, a presentation that may also be carried to millions of people in a television audience and giving a prepared talk, speech, or lecture that is continuous—that is, that lasts for a decent amount of time. When the president of the United States gives his State of the Union address, he is in a large room, speaks for around an hour, and, at the same time, millions of people are watching him carefully on television and listening to what he says on the radio. Most of the time we can assume that public speaking involves face-to-face communication and a prepared, continuous talk.

We must not underestimate the power of a speech. Thus, for example, Barack Obama gave a speech to a Democratic political convention in an auditorium in Boston in 2004 with thousands of people in it; but it was also broadcast on television. And that speech is credited with launching Obama as an important politician and eventually led to him becoming president of the United States.

Aristotle's Rhetoric and Public Speaking

We have already read Aristotle's ideas in his *Rhetoric* about being a persuasive speaker. He also offers advice on how to give speeches (McKeon, 1941):

In making a speech one must study three points: first, the means of producing persuasion; second, the style, or language, to be used; third, the proper arrangement of the various parts of the speech. We have already specified the sources of persuasion. We have shown that they are three in number; what they are; and why there are only these three: for we have shown that persuasion must in every case be effected either (1) by working on the emotions of the judges themselves, (2) by giving them the right impression of the speaker's character, or (3) by proving the truth of the statements made… Our next subject will be the style of expression. For it is not enough to know *what* we ought to say; we must also say it *as* we ought; much help is thus afforded towards producing the right impression. (p. 1434–1435)

Aristotle goes on, at length, about other related matters, such as how to state one's case (the statement) and prove it (the argument), the power of the human voice, and countless other topics. From Aristotle we get a guide to making speeches:

1. Focus on the argument by working on your audience's emotions, maximizing your status as an authority, and using reason and logic to support your case.
2. Pay attention to style—because the language you use and the way you use your voice will have an important effect on your listeners.
3. Consider the arrangement of elements or topics you deal with in your speech. They should follow upon one another in a logical manner, and your conclusion should leave your audience with a sense of accomplishment—of having learned something of value.

Aristotle is working at a high level of abstraction, here, but he does offer us a guide to public speaking. Of course not all public speaking is based on persuasion, but even in speeches that are basically descriptive or explanatory, you still want to interest and entertain your audience and give them a reason to believe that what you are telling them is truthful and useful to them. It also helps if you have an interesting title for your speech. For example, I titled a lecture I gave in Istanbul a number of years ago "The Semiotics of Love," and that attracted a number of people who were intrigued by my title.

Figure 5-1 *Semiotics of Love* Poster

Television Commercials and the Craft of Public Speaking

We can gain some insights into public speaking by taking cues from the best television commercials. These commercials often start in the middle of an action, to make us curious about what is going on, instead of using the old Aristotelian formula of having a beginning, middle, and an end or conclusion. Because audiences don't like being bothered by them, commercials have to attract the attention of television viewers immediately. Then the commercial's goal is to stimulate desire and finally to lead to an action—purchasing some product or service. In speeches, what lecturers seek is "approval" from our audiences—that is, a sense that the time they spent listening to the lecture was worth it. As a public speaker you have an obligation to inform and entertain (in the best sense of the term) your audience. Many communication scholars suggest we think of public speaking as a form of enhanced conversation, though one that is not interactive like personal conversations. That means we should be natural and informal as contrasted with giving an oration.

What I describe as starting in the middle means that when you give a speech, it is important to find something that will make your audience curious about what you are going to talk about. For example, you might start with a story—to get your audience's attention. But it must be relevant to the subject of your talk. Then you can move on to something else, but you must remember to return to the story and tell how it ends and explain how it was relevant. Or you can ask the audience a question to get them thinking or make an outrageous statement that makes them curious.

People are interested in stories and starting with a story is a good way to get an audience's attention. But if your story drags on endlessly, you will lose your audience. You can, of course, start a story and then move onto something else before returning to the story. And, as I just suggested, the story must be tied to the subject of your talk.

The Power of Preparation

There are a number of things you can do to prepare for your speech. One thing I would suggest is to be over-prepared. If you practice your speech a number of times, if you tape it and listen to it, if you feel confident about being able to deliver it in a manner that will appeal to your audience, you'll have no reason to worry. It is natural to be nervous before speaking in public. But if you are well prepared and have practiced your speech enough times, you'll be fine. If you're under-prepared, however, you'll have good reason to be nervous.

There are a number of ways you can practice your speeches. First, you can give your speech in an empty room to get a sense of how it flows. Second, you can tape record your speech to see how you sound and to determine whether your organization and choice of language are effective. You can also practice giving it with some friends and see how they respond to it.

Remember to consider your audience's interests and to tie your talk to them. If your focus is on your audience rather than yourself, you'll soon stop thinking about yourself being in front of them and will see yourself as being part of them. And if you can amuse them at the same time you're doing whatever it is you want to do with your speech, all the better.

It is also useful to visualize your presentation in your mind's eye. Imagine yourself in front of your audience giving your speech. Imagine the audience listening to what you have to say and enjoying your talk. Think about when you'll be pausing, what body movements you might want to make, when to give the audience time to respond to any humor in the speech. Over prepare and you'll do well.

The Need to Focus

It is important to maintain your focus on whatever it is you are talking about. You want to avoid speaking in a discursive style. Discursive speakers digress from the subject of their presentations and talk about all kinds of things tangential or not even related to what they said they would talk about. And often they digress from their digressions. This usually means they lose their audience, who start wondering what's going on.

Keeping focused means that whatever you talk about should be relevant to your main topic. It is also a good idea to be mindful of the flow of your speech. You can also help your audience by giving them transition cues such as, "on the other hand," "in addition," "now we consider," and so on. It also helps if you inject an element of redundancy in your

talks, since some members of your audience may have not paid attention to an important point.

The Art of Being Relevant

Ambrose Beirce, an American humorist known as "Bitter Beirce" because of his hostile aphorisms, described a bore as "someone who talks when you want him to listen." What we learn from Beirce is that people's attention spans are very short and often they may think they know more about what you are talking about than you do. This means we must be relevant to the interests and needs of audiences. We can be relevant when:

Figure 5.2 Discursive Speaker

1. **We show how what we are talking about will affect them.**

   "I'm going to talk about global warming and the impact it will have on your life and your children's lives. And your grandchildren's lives. The extreme weather we've been experiencing in the United States may be indirectly caused by global warming, and as the icecaps in Greenland melt and the level of the seas rise, in the not too distant future you may find that where you are living will be under six feet of water."

2. **We take advantage of their desire for information of use to them.**

   "You can be healthier if you adopt the Mediterranean diet and eat lots of fresh vegetables, such as broccoli and avocados, eat a handful of nuts every day, and use olive oil for your salads. And the wonderful thing about the diet is that it is delicious as well as healthful."

3. **We provide them with information they didn't have.**
"Some adolescents are now sending as many as one hundred text messages a day to their friends. They spend over an hour a day doing so. This means that in the course of a month they send three thousand text messages and spend more than thirty hours doing so. They may be doing physical harm to themselves with repetitive stress injuries, and they also may be doing psychological harm to themselves by distancing themselves from their siblings and parents."

4. **We show relationships between things they didn't recognize.**
"As a result of the popularity of smartphones, the sales of low-end digital cameras have dropped dramatically, and smartphones are also replacing watches for many people. We don't know how many other industries smartphones will disrupt, but there are plenty of presidents of companies that manufacture things that can be replaced by apps on smartphones who have worried looks on their faces."

5. **We offer explanations they find interesting.**
"Freud's theory of the Oedipus complex may explain why children have such powerful hostile feelings toward the parent of the opposite sex when they are young... and sometimes when they are older. His theory about the unconscious also explains why we do things that are irrational and self-destructive. And that is because there is material in our psyches, of which we are unaware, that shapes our behavior."

6. **We are entertaining, which means we may use our own sense of humor or found humor, here and there, in the talk to amuse people.**
"Before I begin my talk on media, I ought to tell you that a reviewer of my book, *The TV-Guided American*, wrote 'Berger is

to the study of television what Idi Amin is to tourism in Uganda.' Since he was murdering hundreds of thousands of people at the time, I have to conclude he didn't like my book." Note: I am quoting here from a review of my book. When I use this quotation in lectures, the audience always has a big laugh (since the review is very insulting). This is an example of what we might call "found humor," in which we use something from the press or some other source in a humorous way. It is not a good idea to start speeches with jokes, because your audience may have already heard the joke, may not think it is funny, and you may not tell jokes well. It is much better to create your own humor, using such techniques as: exaggeration, insult, parody, irony, and so on, or use found humor.

7. **We consider our body language and facial expressions when we talk.**

   "You may notice I have a smile on my face. Ordinarily, I never smile. In fact, I can't remember smiling more than once or twice in the past ten years. (Exaggeration and victim humor.) The reason I'm smiling is because I just learned I've been awarded..."

8. **We use but don't overuse audio-visual techniques to enhance our presentations. Images, as I explained in my discussion of nonverbal communication, are very powerful.**

   You must be judicious with PowerPoint presentations. They are used so often that some companies now prohibit speakers from using presentation media, in part because the speakers often spend their time talking to the images on the screen and not looking at the audience and interacting with it. If you do use presentation software, don't have slides of long passages of words; it is best to have charts, diagrams, and lists that will be useful to you. Make use of the power of images when you use PowerPoint, not the power of words. As I explained earlier, images fascinate people and have the ability to hold their attention.

We do all of the above using, when appropriate, case histories—stories that allow us to keep our audience's interest and, at the same time, teach them something— and, if possible, also entertain them.

The Audience Shapes the Speech

We must remember one of the key rules of public speaking and communication in general: the audience shapes the speech. We have to adapt our talk to the audience we have. Thus, we give different talks to an audience of teenagers than we do to an audience of senior citizens, and the language we use differs when we talk to audiences that are not highly educated and we talk to a room full of professors or people with advanced degrees. In all cases, though, we must assume a certain level of intelligence in our audience and avoid "talking down" to anyone. We use different language, and we adopt a different tone to our talks. Whenever we communicate with others, we have to be able to reach them, and one way we do this is by adopting an appropriate tone and considering their knowledge base. If you are speaking to people who communicate using what Bernstein called "the restricted code," which he described as being the code for working class people and as being grammatically simple, using short sentences and a limited vocabulary, it doesn't make sense to talk to them using "the elaborated code." This doesn't mean you can't deal with complicated topics. It means you have to explain things using relatively simple language.

We must always remember, of course, to avoid language that members of any audience may find distasteful, such as insulting, sexist, racist, anti-Semitic, and other such kinds of speech. Audiences don't like being insulted (unless it is by a comedian, and even then it is dangerous), and there's no reason to do anything to antagonize your audience when speaking. You should avoid vulgar language and slang and a style that is not appropriate to your audience. Your audience will expect you to be giving your speech and not plagiarizing material from someone else. You can borrow material from others; that's perfectly acceptable. But you must give them credit for it. You should mention the authors and their works that you are using. For example, if you are using material from Clotaire Rapaille on imprinting in children, you should say something like, "As the French psychoanalyst and marketing consultant Clotaire Rapaille wrote in *The Culture Code...*," and then quote him or paraphrase him.

Speaking at Different Levels on the Ladder of Abstraction

When we speak, just as we don't want to talk in a monotone, without ever raising our voice or always speaking softly, we also don't want to stay at the same level of abstraction. By this I mean we should make sure that sometimes we give examples of things we are talking about but also sometimes use abstractions to make generalizations. If we only talk about specific things, our talk has no implications and becomes mired in the particular. If we only talk at a high level of abstraction, we seem to lose contact with reality. So we must learn how to move up and down the *ladder of abstraction*. It was the semanticist S. I. Hayakawa who wrote about ladders of abstraction in his book, *Language in Thought and Action*, which went through many editions. Let me offer an example. My ladder starts at the bottom with Rover and moves up the ladder to kinds of dogs to common pets and, finally, to animals of all kinds.

Figure 5-3 The Ladder of Abstraction

Five Tips for Giving Interesting Speeches

Philosophers and others have been writing about rhetoric for thousands of years, and there are a huge number of concepts— with Latin names—that make up the field. Thus, rhetoricians talk about "enantiosis," which means "irony," and "Parataxis," which means "placing side by side." And there are thousands of other terms like the ones I've given.

Cicero (1942), one of the great rhetoricians, wrote, in his *De Oratore*, about the "five parts" or rhetoric:

> Since all the activity and ability of an orator falls into five divisions... he must first hit upon what to say; then manage and marshal his discoveries, not merely in orderly fashion, but with a discriminating eye for the exact weight as it were of each argument; next go on to array them in the adornments of style; after that keep them guarded in his memory; and in the end deliver them with effect and charm. (p. xxxi)

That is, according to Cicero, a speaker must consider:

Inventio	Invention	The content of your speech
Dispositio	Arrangement	How you order the elements in your speech
Elocutio	Style	Your style of speaking
Actio	Delivery	Your use of your voice in speaking
Memoria	Memory	What your audience remembers about your speech

These are the basic components of public speaking and can serve as a kind of summary for you to keep in mind when thinking about your speech. I should add, as a general note, that it is perfectly useful to use the word "I" and personal pronouns like "he" or "she" when you speak. Trying to avoid using "I" and personal pronouns can lead to all kinds of problems and awkward linguistic complications. Using "I" may also help guide you to create a personal style that will make you and your audience more comfortable when you speak.

I offer now five tips, based on the rhetorical principles just discussed, that will help you give strong speeches.

1. Description

This involves how much detail you include in describing things. If you are too general or vague, your audience won't get a good picture of what you're talking about, and if you are too detailed, your audience may lose the thread of your argument or become bored. Think of the difference between saying "I had lunch at Le Meridien" and the kind of description of a typical meal at a good French restaurant found in restaurant reviews in [*The*] *New York Times*. In these reviews, the restaurant critics discuss the atmosphere in the restaurant, the foods served, the specialties of the restaurant, the quality of the cooking, what particular dishes taste like, what dishes were successful and what dishes weren't, and all kinds of other things. People prefer detailed descriptions because it gives them a better sense of what you are talking about.

2. Exemplification

This involves giving examples of whatever it is you are talking about, and going from the general to the specific. For example, if you are talking about how the Supreme Court works, you should then discuss some important cases. Exemplification is a way of moving down the ladder of abstraction from animals in general to Rover, your dog.

3. Explanation

Explanation involves telling your audience things like how some process works or why something happened. This can involve explaining something simple, like the way an Espresso machine works, or complicated, like how Obama won the American presidency or how the Supreme Court makes its decisions. If you talk about a theoretical concept, you should show it can be used to explain something. For example, the concept "obsessive compulsive disorder" helps explain why some people wash their hands two hundred times a day.

4. Figurative Language: Metaphor and Metonymy

There are two kinds of figurative language I wish to focus on here: "metaphor" and "metonymy." I've dealt with them in many places in the book, but primarily in my discussion of semiotic theory. Metaphor, let us recall, is language that uses "is" and compares two things that are alike in some way. It is based on identity. A weaker form of metaphor is called simile and uses "like" or "as" to compare two things. It is based on similarity. For example, [to say] "My love is a rose" is a metaphor and [to say] "My love is *like* a rose" is a simile. Metonymy is based on association, which is used to generate meaning. If we want to suggest wealth in a television commercial, we may show someone in a Rolls Royce automobile. A weaker form of metonymy is called synecdoche, in which a part stands for the whole or vice versa. Thus, we say "The White House" to stand for the presidency and the executive part of the government.

What we must remember is that metaphor and metonym are central to our thinking. As George Lakoff and Mark Johnson (1980) write in their book, *Metaphors We Live By*:

> Most people think they can get along perfectly well without metaphor. We have found, on the contrary, that metaphor is pervasive in everyday life, not just in language but in thought and action. Our ordinary conceptual system, in terms of which we both think and act, is fundamentally metaphoric in nature. (p. 3)

Sometimes something can function both metaphorically and metonymically. Thus, the snake that tempted Eve is both metaphorically a phallic symbol (all snakes are according to Freud) and metonymically something that calls the Garden of Eden to mind.

If people think metaphorically and metonymically (even though most people may never have heard of the terms), it makes good sense to use metaphors and metonyms in your talk. These devices have the power to grab our attention and impress themselves on our memory.

5. Summaries and Conclusions

A summary is a list of all the things you talked about in your speech, given to your audience as an aid to their memory. One of the canons of public speaking is:

> "Tell them what you'll tell them,
> tell them,
> then tell them what you've told them."

But I have suggested that it is a good idea to start in the middle—to get your audience interested—and then tell them what you'll tell them, then tell them what you want to tell them, and then tell them what you told them. If you offer a summary, you can tell them what you've told them.

If, on the other hand, your talk is such that at the end of it you can show where your talk leads and offer a conclusion that is more than just a summary, you'll have offered a much stronger ending to your talk— because your audience will see where your speech has been leading. Your audience will have discovered something and will probably retain the information you provided more than they would if you ended your talk with a summary. You can think of a conclusion as being something like the way a murder is revealed at the end of a mystery. At the end of Agatha Christie's stories with Hercule Poirot, he usually gathers everyone involved in the story together, offers a summary of what happened, and then reveals how the murderer did it and who the murderer is.

Now Go Out and Do It!

It's one thing to learn theories that will help you perform well when public speaking, but all the theories in the world won't help you unless you use them when you give speeches. So it is important that when you practice your speeches, you make sure you've used the material discussed in this chapter to give your speeches richness and personality. Remember, when you prepare for public speaking, if you don't like what you're saying and find your presentation lively and interesting, your audience won't either.

Part II

Crafting Memorable Messages

Audience Analysis

By Jason S. Wrench, Anne Goding, Danette Ifert Johnson, and Bernardo A. Attias

What Is an Audience Analysis?

One of the consequences of the First Amendment to the Constitution, which protects our right to speak freely, is that we focus so much on what we want to say that we often overlook the question of who our audience is. Does your audience care what you as a speaker think? Can they see how your speech applies to their lives and interests? The act of public speaking is a shared activity that involves interaction between speaker and audience. In order for your speech to get a fair hearing, you need to create a relationship with your listeners. Scholars Sprague, Stuart, and Bodary (2000) explain, "Speakers do not give speeches *to* audiences; they jointly create meaning *with* audiences." The success of your speech rests in large part on how your audience receives and understands it.

Think of a time when you heard a speech that sounded "canned" or that fell flat because the audience didn't "get it." Chances are that this happened because the speaker neglected to consider that public speaking is an audience-centered activity. Worse, lack of consideration for one's audience can result in the embarrassment of alienating listeners by telling a joke they don't appreciate, or using language they

find offensive. The best way to reduce the risk of such situations is to conduct an audience analysis as you prepare your speech.

Audience analysis is the process of gathering information about the people in your audience so that you can understand

© *Thinkstock* their needs, expectations, beliefs, values, attitudes, and likely opinions. In this chapter, we will first examine some reasons why audience analysis is important. We will then describe three different types of audience analysis and some techniques to use in conducting audience analysis. Finally, we will explain how you can use your audience analysis not only during the creation of your speech but also while you are delivering it.

Three Types of Audience Analysis

LEARNING OBJECTIVES

1. Understand how to gather and use demographic information.
2. Understand how to gather and use psychographic information.
3. Understand how to gather and use situational information.

While audience analysis does not guarantee against errors in judgment, it will help you make good choices in topic, language, style of presentation, and other aspects of your speech. The more you know about your audience, the better you can serve their interests and needs. There are certainly limits to what we can learn through information collection, and we need to acknowledge that before making assumptions, but knowing how to gather and use information through audience analysis is an essential skill for successful speakers.

Demographic Analysis

As indicated earlier, demographic information includes factors such as gender, age range, marital status, race and ethnicity, and socio-economic status. In your public speaking class, you probably already know how many students are male and female, their approximate ages, and so forth. But how can you assess the demographics of an audience ahead of time if you have had no previous contact with them? In many cases, you can ask the person or organization that has invited you to speak; it's likely that they can tell you a lot about the demographics of the people who are expected to come to hear you.

Whatever method you use to gather demographics, exercise respect from the outset. For instance, if you are collecting information about whether audience members have ever been divorced, be aware that not everyone will want to answer your questions. You can't require them to do so, and you may not make assumptions about their reluctance to discuss the topic. You must allow them their privacy.

Age

There are certain things you can learn about an audience based on age. For instance, if your audience members are first-year college students, you can assume that they have grown up in the post-9/11 era and have limited memory of what life was like before the "war on terror." If your audience includes people in their forties and fifties, it is likely they remember a time when people feared they would contract the AIDS virus from shaking hands or using a public restroom. People who are in their sixties today came of age during the 1960s, the era of the Vietnam War and a time of social confrontation and experimentation. They also have frames of reference that contribute to the way they think, but it may not be easy to predict which side of the issues they support.

Gender

Gender can define human experience. Clearly, most women have had a different cultural experience from that of men within the same culture. Some women have found themselves excluded from certain careers. Some men have found themselves blamed for the limitations imposed on women. In books such as *You Just Don't Understand* and *Talking from 9 to 5*, linguist Deborah Tannen (1994) has written extensively on differences between men's and women's communication styles. Tannen explains,

> This is not to say that all women and all men, or all boys and girls, behave any one way. Many factors influence our styles, including regional and ethnic backgrounds, family experience and individual personality. But gender is a key factor, and understanding its influence can help clarify what happens when we talk.

Marriage tends to impose additional roles on both men and women and divorce even more so, especially if there are children. Even if your audience consists of young adults who have not yet made occupational or marital commitments, they are still aware that gender and the choices they make about issues such as careers and relationships will influence their experience as adults.

Culture

In past generations, Americans often used the metaphor of a "melting pot" to symbolize the assimilation of immigrants from various countries and cultures into a unified, harmonious "American people." Today, we are aware of the limitations in that metaphor, and have largely replaced it with a multiculturalist view that describes the American fabric as a "patchwork" or a "mosaic." We know that people who immigrate do not abandon their cultures of origin in order to conform to a standard American identity. In fact, cultural continuity is now viewed as a healthy source of identity.

We also know that subcultures and cocultures exist within and alongside larger cultural groups. For example, while we are aware that Native American people do not all embrace the same values, beliefs, and customs as mainstream white Americans, we also know that members of the Navajo nation have different values, beliefs, and customs from those of members of the Sioux or the Seneca. We know that African American people in urban centers like Detroit and Boston do not share the same cultural experiences as those living in rural Mississippi. Similarly, white Americans in San Francisco may be culturally rooted in the narrative of distant ancestors from Scotland, Italy, or Sweden or in the experience of having emigrated much more recently from Australia, Croatia, or Poland.

Not all cultural membership is visibly obvious. For example, people in German American and Italian American families have widely different sets of values and practices, yet others may not be able to differentiate members of these groups. Differences are what make each group interesting and are important sources of knowledge, perspectives, and creativity.

Religion

There is wide variability in religion as well. The Pew Forum on Religion and Public Life (2008) found in a nationwide survey that 84 percent of Americans identify with at least one of a dozen major religions, including Christianity, Judaism, Buddhism, Islam, Hinduism, and others. Within Christianity alone, there are half a dozen categories including Roman Catholic, Mormon, Jehovah's Witness, Orthodox (Greek and Russian), and a variety of Protestant denominations. Another 6 percent said they were unaffiliated but religious, meaning that only one American in ten is atheist, agnostic, or "nothing in particular."

Even within a given denomination, a great deal of diversity can be found. For instance, among Roman Catholics alone, there are people who are devoutly religious, people who self-identify as Catholic but do not attend mass or engage in other religious practices, and others who faithfully make confession and attend mass but who openly question Papal doctrine on various issues. Catholicism among immigrants from the Caribbean and Brazil is often blended with indigenous religion or with religion imported from the west coast of Africa. It is very different from Catholicism in the Vatican.

The dimensions of diversity in the religion demographic are almost endless, and they are not limited by denomination. Imagine conducting an audience analysis of people belonging to an individual congregation rather than a denomination: even there, you will most likely find a multitude of variations that involve how one was brought up, adoption of a faith system as an adult, how strictly one observes religious practices, and so on.

Yet, even with these multiple facets, religion is still a meaningful demographic lens. It can be an indicator of probable patterns in family relationships, family size, and moral attitudes.

Group Membership

In your classroom audience alone, there will be students from a variety of academic majors. Every major has its own set of values, goals, principles, and codes of ethics. A political science student preparing for law school might seem to have little in common with a student of music therapy, for instance. In addition, there are other group memberships that influence how audience members understand the world. Fraternities and sororities, sports teams, campus organizations, political parties, volunteerism, and cultural communities all provide people with ways of understanding the world as it is and as we think it should be.

Because public speaking audiences are very often members of one group or another, group membership is a useful and often easy to access facet of audience analysis. The more you know about the associations of your audience members, the better prepared you will be to tailor your speech to their interests, expectations, and needs.

Education

Education is expensive, and people pursue education for many reasons. Some people seek to become educated, while others seek to earn professional credentials. Both are important motivations. If you know the education levels attained by members of your audience, you might not know their motivations, but you will know to what extent they could somehow afford the money for an education, afford the time to get an education, and survive educational demands successfully.

The kind of education is also important. For instance, an airplane mechanic undergoes a very different kind of education and training from that of an accountant or a software engineer. This means that not only the attained level of education but also the particular field is important in your understanding of your audience.

Occupation

People choose occupations for reasons of motivation and interest, but their occupations also influence their perceptions and their interests. There are many misconceptions about most occupations. For instance, many people believe that teachers work an eight-hour day and have summers off. When you ask teachers, however, you might be surprised to find out that they take work home with them for evenings and weekends, and during the summer, they may teach summer school as well as taking courses in order to keep up with new developments in their fields. But even if you don't know those things, you would still know that teachers have had rigorous generalized and specialized qualifying education, that they have a complex set of responsibilities in the classroom and the institution, and that, to some extent, they have chosen a relatively low-paying occupation over such fields as law, advertising, media, fine and performing arts, or medicine. If your audience includes doctors and nurses, you know that you are speaking to people with differing but important philosophies of health and illness. Learning about those occupational realities is important in avoiding wrong assumptions and stereotypes. We insist that you not assume that nurses are merely doctors "lite." Their skills, concerns, and responsibilities are almost entirely different, and both are crucially necessary to effective health care.

Psychographic Analysis

Earlier, we mentioned psychographic information, which includes such things as values, opinions, attitudes, and beliefs. Authors Grice and Skinner (2009) present a model in which values are the basis for beliefs, attitudes, and behaviors. Values are the foundation of their pyramid model. They say,

> A value expresses a judgment of what is desirable and undesirable, right and wrong, or good and evil. Values are usually stated in the form of a word or phrase. For example, most of us probably share the values of equality, freedom, honesty, fairness, justice, good health, and family. These values compose the principles or standards we use to judge and develop our beliefs, attitudes, and behaviors.

It is important to recognize that, while demographic information is fairly straightforward and verifiable, psychographic information is much less clear-cut. Two different people who both say they believe in equal educational opportunity may have very different interpretations of what "equal opportunity" means. People who say they don't buy junk food may have very different standards for what specific kinds of foods are considered "junk food."

We also acknowledge that people inherit some values from their family upbringing, cultural influences, and life experiences. The extent to which someone values family loyalty and obedience to parents, thrift, humility, and work may be determined by these influences more than by individual choice.

Psychographic analysis can reveal preexisting notions that limit your audience's frame of reference. By knowing about such notions ahead of time, you can address them in your speech. Audiences are likely to have two basic kinds of preexisting notions: those about the topic and those about the speaker.

Preexisting Notions About Your Topic

Many things are a great deal more complex than we realize. Media stereotypes often contribute to our oversimplifications. For instance, one of your authors, teaching public speaking in the past decade, was surprised to hear a student claim that "the hippies meant well, but they did it wrong." Aside from the question of the "it" that was done wrong, there was a question about how little the student actually knew about the diverse hippy cultures and their aspirations. The student seemed unaware that some of "the hippies" were the forebears of such things as organic bakeries, natural food co-ops, urban gardens, recycling, alternative energy, wellness, and other arguably positive developments.

It's important to know your audience in order to make a rational judgment about how their views of your topic might be shaped. In speaking to an audience that might have differing definitions, you should take care to define your terms in a clear, honest way.

At the opposite end from oversimplification is the level of sophistication your audience might embody. Your audience analysis should include factors that reveal it. Suppose you are speaking about trends in civil rights in the United States. You cannot pretend that advancement of civil rights is virtually complete nor can you claim that no progress has been made. It is likely that in a college classroom, the audience will know that although much progress has been made, there are still pockets of prejudice, discrimination, and violence. When you speak to an audience that is cognitively complex, your strategy must be different from one you would use for an audience that is less educated in the topic. With a cognitively complex audience, you must acknowledge the overall complexity while stating that your focus will be on only one dimension. With an audience that's uninformed about your topic, that strategy in a persuasive speech could confuse them; they might well prefer a black-and-white message with no gray areas. You must decide whether it is ethical to represent your topic this way.

When you prepare to do your audience analysis, include questions that reveal how much your audience already knows about your topic. Try to ascertain the existence of stereotyped, oversimplified, or prejudiced attitudes about it. This could make a difference in your choice of topic or in your approach to the audience and topic.

Preexisting Notions About You

People form opinions readily. For instance, we know that students form impressions of teachers the moment they walk into our classrooms on the first day. You get an immediate impression of our age, competence, and attitude simply from our appearance and nonverbal behavior. In addition, many have heard other students say what they think of us.

The same is almost certainly true of you. But it's not always easy to get others to be honest about their impressions of you. They're likely to tell you what they think you want to hear. Sometimes, however, you do know what others think. They might think of you as a jock, a suit-wearing conservative, a nature lover, and so on. Based on these impressions, your audience might expect a boring speech, a shallow speech, a sermon, and so on. However, your concern should still be serving your audience's needs and interests, not debunking their opinions of you or managing your image. In order to help them be receptive, you address their interests directly, and make sure they get an interesting, ethical speech.

Situational Analysis

The next type of analysis is called the situational audience analysis because it focuses on characteristics related to the specific speaking situation. The situational audience analysis can be divided into two main questions:

4. How many people came to hear my speech and why are they here? What events, concerns, and needs motivated them to come? What is their interest level, and what else might be competing for their attention?
5. What is the physical environment of the speaking situation? What is the size of the audience, layout of the room, existence of a podium or a microphone, and availability of digital media for visual aids? Are there any distractions, such as traffic noise?

Audience Size

In a typical class, your audience is likely to consist of twenty to thirty listeners. This audience size gives you the latitude to be relatively informal within the bounds of good judgment. It isn't too difficult to let each audience member feel as though you're speaking to him or her. However, you would not become so informal that you allow your carefully prepared speech to lapse into shallow entertainment. With larger audiences, it's more difficult to reach out to each listener, and your speech will tend to be more formal, staying more strictly within its careful outline. You will have to work harder to prepare visual and audio material that reaches the people sitting at the back of the room, including possibly using amplification.

Occasion

There are many occasions for speeches. Awards ceremonies, conventions and conferences, holidays, and other celebrations are some examples. However, there are also less joyful reasons for a speech, such as funerals, disasters, and the delivery of bad news. As always, there are likely to be mixed reactions. For instance, award ceremonies are good for community and institutional morale, but we wouldn't be surprised to find at least a little resentment from listeners who feel deserving but were overlooked. Likewise, for a speech announcing bad news, it is likely that at least a few listeners will be glad the bad news wasn't even worse. If your speech is to deliver bad news, it's important to be honest but also to avoid traumatizing your audience. For instance, if you are a condominium board member speaking to a residents' meeting after the building was damaged by a hurricane, you will need to provide accurate data about the extent of the damage and the anticipated cost and time required for repairs. At the same time, it would be needlessly upsetting to launch into a graphic description of injuries suffered by people, animals, and property in neighboring areas not connected to your condomium complex.

Some of the most successful speeches benefit from situational analysis to identify audience concerns related to the occasion. For example, when the president of the United States gives the annual State of the Union address, the occasion calls for commenting on the condition of the nation and outlining the legislative agenda for the coming year. The speech could be a formality that would interest only "policy wonks," or with the use of good situational audience analysis, it could be a popular event reinforcing the connection between the president and the American people. In January 2011, knowing that the United States' economy was slowly recovering and that jobless rates were still very high, President Barack Obama and his staff knew that the focus of the speech had to be on jobs. Similarly, in January 2003, President George W. Bush's State of the Union speech focused on the "war on terror" and his reasons for justifying the invasion of Iraq. If you look at the history of State of the Union Addresses, you'll often find that the speeches are tailored to the political, social, and economic situations facing the United States at those times.

Voluntariness of Audience

A voluntary audience gathers because they want to hear the speech, attend the event, or participate in an event. A classroom audience, in contrast, is likely to be a captive audience. Captive audiences are required to be present or feel obligated to do so. Given the limited choices perceived, a captive audience might give only grudging attention. Even when there's an element of choice, the likely consequences of nonattendance will keep audience members from leaving. The audience's relative perception of choice increases the importance of holding their interest.

Whether or not the audience members chose to be present, you want them to be interested in what you have to say. Almost any audience will be interested in a topic that pertains directly to them. However, your audience might also be receptive to topics that are indirectly or potentially pertinent to their lives. This means that if you choose a topic such as advances in the treatment of spinal cord injury or advances in green technology, you should do your best to show how these topics are potentially relevant to their lives or careers.

However, there are some topics that appeal to audience curiosity even when it seems there's little chance of direct pertinence. For instance, topics such as Blackbeard the pirate or ceremonial tattoos among the Maori might pique the interests of various audiences. Depending on the instructions you get from your instructor, you can consider building an interesting message about something outside the daily foci of our attention.

Physical Setting

The physical setting can make or break even the best speeches, so it is important to exercise as much control as you can over it. In your classroom, conditions might not be ideal, but at least the setting is familiar. Still, you know your classroom from the perspective of an audience member, not a speaker standing in the front—which is why you should seek out any opporutunity to rehearse your speech during a minute when the room is empty. If you will be giving your presentation somewhere else, it is a good idea to visit the venue ahead of time if at all possible and make note of any factors that will affect how you present your speech. In any case, be sure to arrive well in advance of your speaking time so that you will have time to check that the microphone works, to test out any visual aids, and to request any needed adjustments in lighting, room ventilation, or other factors to eliminate distractions and make your audience more comfortable.

Conducting Audience Analysis

Now that we have described what audience analysis is and why it is important, let's examine some details of how to conduct it. Exactly how can you learn about the people who will make up your audience?

Direct Observation

One way to learn about people is to observe them. By observing nonverbal patterns of behavior, you can learn a great deal as long as you are careful how you interpret the behaviors. For instance, do people greet each other with a handshake, a hug, a smile, or a nod? Do members of opposite sexes make physical contact? Does the setting suggest more conservative behavior? By listening in on conversations, you can find out the issues that concern people. Are people in the campus center talking about political unrest in the Middle East? About concerns over future Pell Grant funding? We suggest that you consider the ethical dimensions of eavesdropping, however. Are you simply overhearing an open conversation, or are you prying into a highly personal or private discussion?

Interviews and Surveys

Because your demographic analysis will be limited to your most likely audience, your most accurate way to learn about them is to seek personal information through interviews and surveys. An interview is a one-on-one exchange in which you ask questions of a respondent, whereas a survey is a set of questions administered to several—or, preferably, many—respondents. Interviews may be conducted face-to-face, by phone, or by written means, such as texting. They allow more in-depth discussion than surveys, and they are also more time consuming to conduct. Surveys are also sometimes conducted face-to-face or by phone, but online surveys are increasingly common. You may collect and tabulate survey results manually, or set up an automated online survey through the free or subscription portals of sites like Survey Monkey and Zoomerang. Using an online survey provides the advantage of keeping responses anonymous, which may increase your audience members' willingness to participate and to answer personal questions. Surveys are an efficient way to collect information quickly; however, in contrast to interviews, they don't allow for follow-up questions to help you understand why your respondent gave a certain answer.

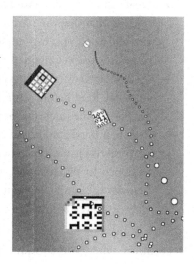

© *Thinkstock*

When you use interviews and surveys, there are several important things to keep in mind:

- Make sure your interview and survey questions are directly related to your speech topic. Do not use interviews to delve into private areas of people's lives. For instance, if your speech is about the debate between creationism and evolution, limit your questions to their opinions about that topic; do not meander into their beliefs about sexual behavior or their personal religious practices.

- Create and use a standard set of questions. If you "ad lib" your questions so that they are phrased differently for different interviewees, you will be comparing "apples and oranges" when you compare the responses you've obtained.
- Keep interviews and surveys short, or you could alienate your audience long before your speech is even outlined. Tell them the purpose of the interview or survey and make sure they understand that their participation is voluntary.
- Don't rely on just a few respondents to inform you about your entire audience. In all likelihood, you have a cognitively diverse audience. In order to accurately identify trends, you will likely need to interview or survey at least ten to twenty people.

In addition, when you conduct interviews and surveys, keep in mind that people are sometimes less than honest in describing their beliefs, attitudes, and behavior. This widely recognized weakness of interviews and survey research is known as *socially desirable responding*: the tendency to give responses that are considered socially acceptable. Marketing professor Ashok Lalwani (2009) divides socially desirable responding into two types: (1) impression management, or intentionally portraying oneself in a favorable light and (2) self-deceptive enhancement, or exaggerating one's good qualities, often unconsciously.

You can reduce the effects of socially desirable responding by choosing your questions carefully. As marketing consultant Terry Vavra (2009) advises, "one should never ask what one can't logically expect respondents to honestly reveal." For example, if you want to know audience members' attitudes about body piercing, you are likely to get more honest answers by asking "Do you think body piercing is attractive?" rather than "How many piercings do you have and where on your body are they located?"

Focus Groups

A focus group is a small group of people who give you feedback about their perceptions. As with interviews and surveys, in a focus group you should use a limited list of carefully prepared questions designed to get at the information you need to understand their beliefs, attitudes, and values specifically related to your topic.

If you conduct a focus group, part of your task will be striking a balance between allowing the discussion to flow freely according to what group members have to say and keeping the group focused on the questions. It's also your job to guide the group in maintaining responsible and respectful behavior toward each other.

In evaluating focus group feedback, do your best to be receptive to what people had to say, whether or not it conforms to what you expected. Your purpose in conducting the group was to understand group members' beliefs, attitudes, and values about your topic, not to confirm your assumptions.

Using Existing Data About Your Audience

Occasionally, existing information will be available about your audience. For instance, if you have a student audience, it might not be difficult to find out what their academic majors are. You might also be able to find out their degree of investment in their educations; for instance, you could reasonably assume that the seniors in the audience have been successful students who have invested at least three years pursuing a higher education. Sophomores have at least survived their first year but may not have matched the seniors in demonstrating strong values toward education and the work ethic necessary to earn a degree.

In another kind of an audience, you might be able to learn other significant facts. For instance, are they veterans? Are they retired teachers? Are they members of a voluntary civic organization such as the Lions Club or Mothers Against Drunk Driving (MADD)? This kind of information should help you respond to their concerns and interests.

In other cases, you may be able to use demographics collected by public and private organizations. Demographic analysis is done by the US Census Bureau through the American Community Survey, which is conducted every year, and through other specialized demographic surveys. The Census Bureau analysis generally captures information about people in all the regions of the United States, but you can drill down in census data to see results by state, by age group, by gender, by race, and by other factors.

Demographic information about narrower segments of the United States, down to the level of individual zip codes, is available through private organizations such as The Nielsen Company, Sperling's Best Places, and Point2Homes. Sales and marketing professionals use this data, and you may find it useful for your audience analysis as well.

KEY TAKEAWAYS

- Several options exist for learning about your audience, including direct observation, interviews, surveys, focus groups, and using existing research about your audience.
- In order to create effective tools for audience analysis, interview and survey questions must be clear and to the point, focus groups must be facilitated carefully, and you must be aware of multiple interpretations of direct observations or existing research about your audience.

Using Your Audience Analysis

LEARNING OBJECTIVES

1. Understand how you can use your audience analysis when you prepare a speech.
2. Recognize how your audience analysis can help you alter your speech while speaking.

A good audience analysis takes time, thought, preparation, implementation, and processing. If done well, it will yield information that will help you interact effectively with your audience. Professional speakers, corporate executives, sales associates, and entertainers all rely on audience analysis to connect with their listeners. So do political candidates, whose chances of gaining votes depend on crafting the message and mood to appeal to each specific audience. One audience might be preoccupied with jobs, another with property taxes, and another with crime. Similarly, your audience analysis should help you identify the interests of your audience. Ultimately, a successful audience analysis can guide you in preparing the basic content of your speech and help you adjust your speech "on the fly."

Prepare Content with Your Audience in Mind

The first thing a good audience analysis can do is help you focus your content for your specific audience. If you are planning on delivering a persuasive speech on why people should become vegans and you find out through analysis that half of your audience are daughters and sons of cattle ranchers, you need to carefully think through your approach to the content. Maybe you'll need to tweak your topic to focus on just the benefits of veganism without trying to persuade the audience explicitly. The last thing you want to do as a speaker is stand before an audience who is highly negative toward your topic before you ever open your mouth. While there will always be some naysayers in any audience, if you think through your topic with your audience in mind, you may be able to find a topic that will be both interesting to you as a speaker and beneficial to your audience as well.

In addition to adjusting the topic of your speech prior to the speaking event, you can also use your audience analysis to help ensure that the content of your speech will be as clear and understandable as humanly possible. We can use our audience analysis to help ensure that we are clear.

One area of clarity to be careful of is the use of idioms your audience may not know. An idiom is a word or phrase where the meaning cannot be predicted from normal, dictionary definitions. Many idioms are culturally or temporally based. For example, the phrase "according to Hoyle" indicates that something is done "by the book" or "by the rules," as in "These measurements aren't according to Hoyle, but they're close enough to give a general idea." Most of us have no clue who Hoyle was or what this idiom means. It refers to Edmond Hoyle, who wrote some of

the most popular card-playing rule books back in the 1700s in England. Today, card game enthusiasts may understand the intent of "according to Hoyle," but for most people it no longer carries specific meaning. When thinking about your speech, be careful not to accidentally use idioms that you find commonplace but your audience may not.

Adjusting Your Speech Based on Your Analysis

In addition to using audience analysis to help formulate speech content, we can also use our audience analysis to make adjustments during the actual speech. These adjustments can pertain to the audience and to the physical setting.

The feedback you receive from your audience during your speech is a valuable indication of ways to adjust your presentation. If you're speaking after lunch and notice audience members looking drowsy, you can make adjustments to liven up the tone of your speech. You could use humor. You could raise your voice slightly. You could pose some questions and ask for a show of hands to get your listeners actively involved. As another example, you may notice from frowns and headshaking that some listeners aren't convinced by the arguments you are presenting. In this case, you could spend more time on a specific area of your speech and provide more evidence than you originally intended. Good speakers can learn a lot by watching their audience while speaking and then make specific adjustments to both the content and delivery of the speech to enhance the speech's ultimate impact.

The second kind of adjustment has to do with the physical setting for your speech. For example, your situational analysis may reveal that you'll be speaking in a large auditorium when you had expected a nice, cozy conference room. If you've created visual aids for a small, intimate environment, you may have to omit it, or tell your listeners that they can view it after the presentation. You may also need to account for a microphone. If you're lucky enough to have a cordless microphone, then you won't have to make too many adjustments to your speaking style. If, on the other hand, the microphone is corded or is attached to an unmovable podium, you'll have to make adjustments to how you deliver the presentation.

In preparing a speech about wealth distribution in the United States, one of our students had the opposite problem. Anticipating a large room, she had planned to use a one-hundred-foot tape measure to illustrate the percentage of the nation's wealth owned by the top one-fifth of the population. However, when she arrived she found that the room was only twelve by twenty feet, so that she had to walk back and forth zigzagging the tape from end to end to stretch out one hundred feet. Had she thought more creatively about how to adapt to the physical setting, she could have

KEY TAKEAWAYS

- You can use your audience analysis to provide you further information about what types of content would be appropriate and meaningful for your specific audience.
- You can use your audience analysis to help you make adjustments to your speech in terms of both how you present the speech within a given environment and also how you adapt your content and delivery based on audience feedback during the speech.

changed her plans to use just ten feet of the tape measure to symbolize 100 percent of the wealth.

References

Bureau of the Census. (2011a). About the American community survey. Retrieved from http://www.census.gov/acs/www/about_the_survey/american_community_survey/

Bureau of the Census. (2011b). Demographic surveys. Retrieved from http://www.census.gov/aboutus/sur_demo.html

Grice, G. L., & Skinner, J. F. (2009). *Mastering public speaking: The handbook* (7th ed.). Boston, MA: Pearson.

Lalwani, A. K. (2009, August). The distinct influence of cognitive busyness and need for closure on cultural differences in socially desirable responding. *Journal of Consumer Research, 36*, 305–316. Retrieved from http://business.utsa.edu/marketing/files/phdpapers/lalwani2_2009-jcr.pdf

Pew Forum on Religion & Public Life. (2008, February). Summary of key findings. In *U.S. religious landscape survey*. Retrieved from http://religions.pewforum.org/reports#

Sprague, J., Stuart, D., & Bodary, D. (2010). *The speaker's handbook* (9th ed.). Boston, MA: Wadsworth Cengage.

Tannen, D. (1994, December 11). The talk of the sandbox: How Johnny and Suzy's playground chatter prepares them for life at the office. *The Washington Post*. Retrieved from http://www9.georgetown.edu/faculty/tannend/sandbox.htm

Vavra, T. G. (2009, June 14). Retrieved from http://www.terryvavra.com/customer-research/the-truth-about-truth-in-survey-research

Demographic Surveys

The Nielsen Company (http://www.nielsen.com)

Sperling's Best Places (http://www.bestplaces.net)

Point2Homes (http://homes.point2.com)

Using Language Well

By E. Michele Ramsey

Introduction

The Power of Language

Imagine for a moment that you were asked to list everything that you know about the country of Italy in spite of the fact that you have never actually visited the country. What would you write? You would have to think about all that you were told about Italy throughout your life, and you would probably list first the bits of information that have been repeated to you by various people and in a variety of contexts. So, for example, you might recall that in geography class you learned particular things about Italy. You might also recall the various movies you've seen that were either supposedly set in Italy or dealt with some element of what has been deemed by the film as "Italian culture." Those movies could include

The Godfather, The Italian Job, or *The DaVinci Code.* You might think about stories your Italian grandmother told you about her childhood spent in Rome or remember images you have seen in history books about World War II. In other words, throughout your life you have learned a lot of different things that you now assume to be true about this country called "Italy" and you've learned all of these things about Italy through language, whether it be through verbal storytelling or through your interpretation of images in a book or on a screen. Now, consider for a moment the possibility that everything you've

heard about Italy has been incorrect. Since you have not ever actually been to the country and had first-hand experience with its geography and culture, for example, how would you know if what you've been told is true or not?

Your purpose is to make your audience see what you saw, hear what you heard, feel what you felt. Relevant detail, couched in concrete, colorful language, is the best way to recreate the incident as it happened and to picture it for the audience.

*~ **Dale Carnegie***

Language is one of the most influential and powerful aspects of our daily lives and yet very few people pay attention to it in their interpersonal and public communication. *The power of language cannot be overemphasized—language constructs, reflects, and maintains our social realities, or what we believe to be "true" with regard to the world around us.* The point of the example above is that what we "know is true" about a person, place, thing, idea, or any other aspect of our daily lives very much depends on what experiences we have had (or not), what information we have (or have not) come across, and what words people have used (or not used) when communicating about our world.

> *Language is a process of free creation; its laws and principles are fixed, but the manner in which the principles of generation are used is free and infinitely varied. Even the interpretation and use of words involves a process of free creation.*
>
> **~ Noam Chomsky**

Language can also have an impact on how we feel about this reality. How we define words and how we feel about those words is highly subjective. In fact, cognitive psychologist Lera Boroditsky showed a key to a group of Spanish-speakers and to a group of German-speakers. The researchers then asked the participants to describe the key they had been shown. Because the Spanish word for "key" is gendered as feminine, Spanish speakers defined the key using words such as lovely, tiny, and magic. The German word for "key" is gendered masculine, however, and German speakers defined the key using adjectives like hard, jagged, and awkward (Boroditsky as cited in Thomas et al., 2003). This study suggests that the words we use to define something can have an impact on how we perceive what those words represent.

Because language is such a powerful, yet unexamined, part of our lives, this chapter focuses on how language functions and how competent speakers harness the power of language.

Consider the case of the Reverend Dr. Martin Luther King, Jr. Indeed, many speakers before him made the very same persuasive arguments regarding the lack of civil rights for Black Americans,

yet we regularly point to the Reverend Dr. King as a preeminent speaker for the civil rights movement because he was a master of language—he employed the power of language to move his audiences in ways they had not been moved before, and we remember him for his eloquence.

Communication vs. Language

To understand the power of language, we need to differentiate between communication and language. **Communication** occurs when we try to transfer what is in our minds to the minds of our audience. Whether speaking to inform, persuade, or entertain, the main goal of a speaker is to effectively communicate her or his thoughts to audience members. Most chapters in this text help you determine how best to communicate information through considerations such as organizational structure, audience analysis, delivery, and the like. **Language**, on the other hand, is the means by which we communicate—a system of symbols we use to form messages. We learn language as a child in order to read, write, and speak. Once we have mastered enough language we can communicate with relative ease, yet growing up we rarely learn much about language choices and what they mean for our communication. We regularly hear people say, "If we just communicated more or for longer periods of time we'd better understand each other." What these types of statements reflect is our lack of understanding of the differences between communication and language. Therefore, many of us believe that when problems arise we should strive to have *more communication* between the parties. But what we need is *better communication* by focusing on language choice.

Language Creates Social Reality

Our social realities are constructed through language; and therefore, people with different experiences in, and understandings of, the world can define the same things in very different ways. Language is culturally transmitted—we learn how to define our world first from our families and then our later definitions of the world are influenced by friends and institutions such as the media, education, and religion. If we grow up in a sexist culture, we are likely to hold sexist attitudes. Similarly, if we grow up in a culture that defines the environment as our first priority in making any decisions, we're likely to grow with environmentally friendly attitudes. Language, then, is not neutral. As a culture, as groups of people, and as individuals, we decide what words we're going to use to define one thing or another.

> *Culture is the collective programming of the mind that distinguishes the members of one category of people from another.*
> ~ **Geert Hofstede**

For public speakers, these facts are important for three primary reasons. First, the careful use of language can make the difference between you giving a remarkable speech and one that is utterly forgettable. Second, you must remember that audience members may not share the same language for the definition of the very same ideas, realities, or even specific items. Finally, the language that you use in public (and even private) communication says something about you—about how you define and therefore perceive the world. If you are not careful with your language you may unintentionally communicate something negative about yourself simply because of a careless use of language. You should think very carefully about your audience's and your own language when you prepare to speak publicly. You can master all of the other elements in this textbook, but without an effective use of language those other mastered skills will not mean much to your audience. The suggestions in this chapter will help you communicate as effectively as possible using appropriate and expressive. You'll also learn about language to avoid so that your language leaves the audience with a positive impression of you.

The Differences Language Choices Can Make

When I discuss the importance of language choice with my students, I generally begin with two different paragraphs based on a section from Reverend Jesse Jackson's "Rainbow Coalition" speech. The first paragraph I read them is a section of Reverend Jackson's speech that I have rewritten. The second paragraph is the actual text from Reverend Jackson's speech. Let's start with my version first:

> America should dream. Choose people over building bombs. Destroy the weapons and don't hurt the people. Think about a new system of values. Think about lawyers more interested in the law than promotions. Consider doctors more interested in helping people get better than in making money. Imagine preachers and priests who will preach and not just solicit money.

This paragraph is clear and simple. It gets the point across to the audience. But compare my version of his paragraph to Reverend Jackson's actual words:

> Young America dream. Choose the human race over the nuclear race. Bury the weapons and don't burn the people. Dream of a new value system. Dream of lawyers more concerned about justice than a judgeship. Dream of doctors more concerned about public health than personal wealth. Dream of preachers and priests who will prophecy and not just profiteer.

The significant difference between these two versions of the paragraph can be explained simply as the difference between carefully choosing one group of words over another group of words. My version of the speech is fine, but it is utterly forgettable. Reverend Jackson's exact wording, however, is stunning. The audience probably remembered his speech and the chills that went down their spines when they heard it long after it was over. This example, I hope, exemplifies the difference language choice can make. Using language in a way that makes you and your speech memorable, however, takes work. Few people come by this talent naturally, so give yourself plenty of time to rework your first draft to fine tune and perfect your language choice. Using some of the strategies discussed below will help you in this process.

Constructing Clear and Vivid Messages

Use Simple Language

When asked to write a speech or a paper, many of us pull out the thesaurus (or call it up on our computer) when we want to replace a common word with one that we believe is more elevated or intellectual. There are certainly times when using a thesaurus is a good thing, but if you're pulling that big book out to turn a simple idea into one that *sounds* more complex, put it back on the shelf. Good speakers use simple language for two primary reasons.

First, audiences can sense a fake. When you turn in your term paper with words that aren't typically used by people in everyday conversation and those words are simply replacing the common words we all use, your instructor knows what you've done. Part of having strong credibility as a speaker is convincing your audience of your sincerity, both in terms of your ideas and your character. When you elevate your language simply for the sake of using big words when small words will do, audiences may perceive you as insincere, and that perception might also transfer onto your message. In addition, the audience's attention can drift to questions about your character and veracity, making it less likely that they are paying attention to your message.

Second, using a long word when a short one will do inhibits your ability to communicate clearly. Your goal as a speaker should be to be as clear as you possibly can. Using language that makes it more difficult for your audience to understand your message can negatively impact your ability to get a clear message across to your audience. If your audience can't understand your vocabulary, they can't understand your message.

A good example of a speaker whose communication was obstructed by language use is Former Secretary of State Alexander Haig. Some examples of his problematic language choice include: "careful caution," "epistemologically wise," "exacerbating restraint," "saddle myself with a statistical fence," and "definitizing an answer" ("Haigledygook and Secretaryspeak," 1981). Chances are good that after reading these phrases over and over you still don't understand him. You can imagine

how much harder it would be to understand Haig's message as it was *delivered orally*—spoken in an instant and then gone! Haig's language clouds rather than clarifies ideas, but it is easy to make sure your message gets across to the audience by avoiding big words that are not necessary.

If you're paying attention to the language strategies discussed in this chapter, you'll find that you won't need to pull out that thesaurus to impress your audience—your command of language will make that positive impression for you. In addition, when you use language that your audience expects to hear and is used to hearing you may find that the audience perceives you as more sincere than someone who uses elevated language and sounds pretentious. Remember: It is rarely the case that you should use a long word when a short one will do.

Most of the fundamental ideas of science are essentially simple, and may, as a rule, be expressed in a language comprehensible to everyone.

~ Albert Einstein

Use Concrete and Precise Language

How many times a week do you say something to someone only to have them misunderstand? You believe that you were very clear and the person you were talking to thought that she understood you perfectly, and yet you both ended up with a problem we often deem "miscommunication." You said you'd "call later" and your friend got angry because you didn't. By "later" you probably meant one time frame while your friend defined that time frame very differently. Often in these cases both people are right. You *were* perfectly clear and your friend *did* understand you perfectly—so how did the miscommunication happen?

One of the primary reasons we miscommunicate is because language is an abstract phenomenon. Meanings exist in people's understandings, not the words we use. Therefore, if you're telling a story about "a dog" you could be talking about a German Shepherd while the person you're talking with is envisioning a Chihuahua. If you do not use concrete language, you risk at least sending a weaker or different message than you intended. When speaking, you want to use the concrete term "German shepherd" over the more abstract term "dog."

When you are writing your speech, look for words that you might need to define more clearly. Instead of talking about "bad weather," tell the audience that it was raining or that hail the size of golf balls was coming down. "Bad weather" means different things to different people. In discussing the aftermath of a natural disaster, rather than saying "a lot of people were affected" say, "25,000 citizens, 1 in every 5, were affected by this disaster." "A lot" means different things to different people. *Most words* mean different things to different people, so use concrete language over abstract words to better your chances of communicating your message as intended.

You also want to make sure that you're precise. Someone might call a sweater "green" while someone else calls it "teal." Even though those are just differences in perception not purposeful or mindless communication meant to be inaccurate, not being clear about exactly which color you're talking about can lead to confusion. It is best to remember to be as precise as possible when choosing words. Don't say something was "big"—tell us its weight or height, and to be sure you're communicating clearly compare that weigh or height to something we understand. So, instead of saying "The piles of garbage I saw in the local dump were really big" say "The piles of garbage I saw in the local dump weighed about 10,000 pounds, which is equivalent to the weight of the average female elephant." The more precise you are the less likely it is that your audience will misinterpret your message.

Our business is infested with idiots who try to impress by using pretentious jargon.

~ David Ogilvy

Another way to avoid language that obstructs communication is to avoid the use of **jargon**. Jargon is the "specialized language of a group or profession" (Hamilton, 2008, p. 286). It is appropriate to use jargon when you know that your audience understands the terms you are using. For example, if you are a computer science major and you are presenting to a group of similarly trained computer science majors, using jargon will help establish your credibility with that audience. Using terms even as basic as "RAM" and "binary code" with a general audience, however, will likely not go over well—you risk confusing the audience rather than informing or persuading them. Even people who can use computers may not know how they work or the technical terms associated with them. So you must be careful to only use jargon when you know your audience will understand it. If you must use jargon while speaking to a general audience, be sure to define your terms and err on the side of over-clarification.

Slang is a language that rolls up its sleeves, spits on its hands and goes to work.

~ Carl Sandburg

Finally, another way to avoid confusion is to avoid using slang when it is not appropriate. **Slang** is language that some people might understand but that is not considered acceptable in formal or polite conversation. Slang may be a poor choice for a speaker because some members of your audience may not be familiar with the slang term(s) you use. Slang is often based in a very specific audience, defined by age, region, subculture and the like. If you are speaking to an audience that you know will understand and respond positively, you may choose to include that language in your speech. Otherwise, do not use slang, or you may confuse and frustrate audience members and cause them to lose interest in your speech. In addition, because slang is often not considered appropriate in formal and polite conversation, using it in your speech may communicate negative ideas about you to audience members.

Don't let a mindless use of slang negatively impact your audience's perception of you and your message.

Using Stylized Language

Stylized language is language that communicates your meaning clearly, vividly and with flair. Stylized language doesn't just make you sound better; it also helps make your speeches more memorable. Speakers who are thoughtful about using language strategies in their speeches are more memorable as speakers and therefore so too are their messages more unforgettable as well.

Metaphors and Similes

One strategy that promotes vivid language is the use of metaphors. **Metaphors** are comparisons made by speaking of one thing in terms of another. **Similes** are similar to metaphors in how they function; however, similes make comparisons by using the word "like" or "as," whereas metaphors do not. The power of a metaphor is in its ability to create an image that is linked to emotion in the mind of the audience. It is one thing to talk about racial injustice, it is quite another for the Reverend Dr. Martin Luther King, Jr. to note that people have been "… battered by storms of persecution and staggered by the winds of police brutality." Throughout his "I Have a Dream" speech the Reverend Dr. King uses the metaphor of the checking account to make his point. He notes that the crowd has come to the March on Washington to "cash a check" and claims that America has "defaulted on this promissory note" by giving "the Negro people a bad check, a check that has come back "insufficient funds." By using checking and bank account terms that most people are familiar with, the Reverend Dr. King is able to more clearly communicate what he believes has occurred. In addition, the use of this metaphor acts as a sort of "shortcut." He gets his point across very quickly by comparing the problems of civil rights to the problems of a checking account.

In the same speech the Reverend Dr. King also makes use of similes, which also compare two things but do so using "like" or "as." In discussing his goals for the Civil Rights movement in his "I Have a Dream" speech, the Reverend Dr. exclaims: "No, no we are not satisfied and we will not be satisfied until justice rolls down like waters and righteousness like a mighty stream." Similes also help make your message clearer by using ideas that are more concrete for your audience. For example, to give the audience an idea of what a winter day looked like you could note that the "snow looked as solid as pearls." To communicate sweltering heat you could say that "the tar on the road looked like satin." A simile most of us are familiar with is the notion of the United States being "like a melting pot" with regard to its diversity. We also often note that a friend or colleague that stays out of conflicts between friends is "like Switzerland." In each of these instances similes have been used to more clearly and vividly communicate a message.

Metaphors have a way of holding the most truth in the least space.

~ Orson Scott Card

Alliteration

Remember challenging yourself or a friend to repeat a tongue twister "five times fast?" Perhaps it was "Sally sold seashells by the seashore" or "Peter Piper picked a peck of pickled peppers." Tongue twisters are difficult to say to say but very easy to remember. Why? Alliteration. **Alliteration** is the repetition of the initial sounds of words. Alliteration is a useful tool for helping people remember your message, and it's as simple as taking a few minutes to see if there are ways to reword your speech so that you can add some alliteration— *this* is a great time to use that thesaurus we talked about putting away early in this chapter. Look for alternative words to use that allow for alliteration in your speech. You might consider doing this especially when it comes to the points that you would like your audience to remember most.

The soul selects her own society.

~ **Emily Dickinson**

Antithesis

Antithesis allows you to use contrasting statements in order to make a rhetorical point. Perhaps the most famous example of antithesis comes from the Inaugural Address of President John F. Kennedy when he stated, "And so, my fellow Americans, ask not what your country can do for you; ask what you can do for your country." Going back to Reverend Jackson's "Rainbow Coalition" speech he notes, "I challenge them to put hope in their brains and not dope in their veins." In each of these cases, the speakers have juxtaposed two competing ideas in one statement to make an argument in order to draw the listener's attention.

You're easy on the eyes—hard on the heart.

~ **Terri Clark**

Parallel Structure and Language

Antithesis is often worded using parallel structure or language. Parallel structure is the balance of two or more similar phrases or clauses, and parallel wording is the balance of two or more similar words. The Reverend Dr. King's "I Have a Dream" speech exemplifies both strategies in action. Indeed, the section where he repeats "I Have a Dream" over and over again is an example of the use of both parallel structure and language. The use of parallel structure and language helps your audience remember without beating them over the head with repetition. If worded and delivered carefully, you can communicate a main point over and over again, as did the Reverend Dr. King, and it doesn't seem as though you are simply repeating the same phrase over and over. You are often doing just that, of course, but because you are careful with your wording (it should be powerful and creative, not pedantic) and your delivery (the correct use of pause, volumes, and other elements of delivery), the audience often perceives the repetition as dramatic and memorable. The use of parallel language and structure can also help you when you are speaking persuasively. Through the use of these strategies you can create a speech that takes your audience through a series of ideas or arguments that seem to "naturally" build to your conclusion.

Personalized Language

We're all very busy people. Perhaps you've got work, studying, classes, a job, and extracurricular activities to juggle. Because we are all so busy, one problem that speakers often face is trying to get their audience interested in their topic or motivated to care about their argument. A way to help solve this problem is through the use of language that personalizes your topic. Rather than saying, "One might argue" say "You might argue." Rather than saying "This could impact the country in ways we have not yet imagined," say "This could impact *your* life in ways that *you* have not imagined." By using language that directly connects your topic or argument to the audience you better your chances of getting your audience to listen and to be persuaded that your subject matter is serious and important to them. Using words like "us," "you," and "we" can be a subtle means of getting your audience to pay attention to your speech. Most people are most interested in things that they believe impact their lives directly—make those connections clear for your audience by using personal language.

The Importance of Ethical and Accurate Language

Language and Ethics

As was noted at the beginning of this chapter, language is culturally transmitted—we learn our language from those around us. For most of us this means that we may first learn language from our parents, but as we grow older, other family members, friends, educators and even the media impact our vocabularies and our choices regarding what language we use. Think about a world without language. Quite simply, we'd have no way of participating in our world without it. People constantly produce language to categorize and organize the world.

Think back to our discussion of how language influences your social reality. In my work as a mentor, I tutored a girl in elementary school who had a very difficult time saying the word "lake." I used the word "lake" as part of a homework exercise. What I had not realized was that she had never seen a lake, either in person or in a picture, or, if she had seen a lake no one had pointed to that body of water and called it a "lake." The concept of a "lake" was simply not in *her* reality. No "lakes" existed in <u>her</u> world. This is a key example of how the language that we learn and that we choose to use says something about our social reality.

Consider the above example another way. Let's say that my young friend had seen a lake and knew how to say the word and what the word referred to, but that she had only been privy to people who used the word negatively. If throughout her life "lakes" were discussed as "bad things" to be avoided, she would have a very different perspective on lakes than most people. Switching this example around a little helps illustrate the fact that language is not neutral. Language carries ideas, and while there is often more than one choice in terms of which word to use, often the words from which you are choosing are not equal in terms of the reality that they communicate.

Think about the difference between calling a specific place "the projects" versus calling that same place "public housing." Both phrases refer to a particular geographical space, but calling a neighborhood "the projects" as opposed to "public housing" communicates something very different, and more negative, about this neighborhood. Often students use the words that they hear more commonly used, so referring to "the projects" as opposed to "public housing" usually indicates that they have not thought enough about their word choices or thought about the impact of those choices.

> *By and large, language is a tool for concealing the truth.*
> ~ **George Carlin**

As this example points out, we have a variety of words from which to choose when constructing a message. Successful speakers recognize that in addition to choosing words that help with clarity and vividness, it is important to think about the connotations associated with one word or the other. When speakers are not careful in terms of word choice in this sense, it is possible to lose credibility with the audience and to create the perception that you are someone that perhaps you are not. If you use "the projects" instead of "public housing," audience members may view you as someone who has negative perceptions of people who live in public housing when you do not feel that way at all. Clearly, not being careful about language choices can be a costly mistake.

But what do these examples have to do with ethics? For our purposes here, there are two ways to think about communication and ethics. First, ethical communication is that which does not unfairly label one thing or another based on personal bias. So, in addition to choosing "public housing" over "the projects," an ethical speaker will choose terms that steer clear from intentional bias. For example, pro-life speakers would refrain from calling "pro-choice" people "pro-abortion" since the basic principle of the "pro-choice" position is that it is up to the person, not society, to choose whether or not an abortion is acceptable. That is a very different position than being "pro-abortion." Indeed, many pro-choice citizens would not choose abortion if faced with an unplanned pregnancy; therefore calling them "pro-abortion" does not reflect the reality of the situation; rather, it is the purposeful and unethical use of one term over the other for emotional impact. Similarly, if a pro-choice person is addressing a crowd where religious organizations are protesting against the legality of abortion, it would not be ethical for the pro-choice speaker to refer to the "antiabortion" protestors as "religious fanatics." Simply because someone is protesting abortion on religious grounds does not make that person a "religious fanatic," and as in the first example, choosing the latter phrase is another purposeful and unethical use of one term over another for emotional impact.

Language exerts hidden power, like the moon on the tides.
~ **Rita Mae Brown**

A second way to link communication and ethics is to remember that ethical speakers attempt to communicate reality to the best of their ability. Granted, as was noted above, each person's social reality is different, depending on background, influences, and cultural institutions, for example. But regardless of whether you think that a "lake" is a good or bad thing, lakes still exist in reality. Regardless of whether or not you think rocks are useful or not, rocks still exist. So ethical communication also means trying to define or explain your subject in terms that are as closely tied to an objective reality as is possible—it is your best attempt to communicate accurately about your topic. Sexist and heterosexist language are two types of language to be avoided by ethical speakers because each type of language does communicate inaccuracies to the audience.

Sexist and Heterosexist Language

One of the primary means by which speakers regularly communicate inaccurate information is through the use of **sexist language**. In spite of the fact that the Modern Language Association deemed sexist language as grammatically incorrect back in the 1970s, many people and institutions (including most colleges and universities) still regularly use sexist language in their communication.

An argument I regularly hear from students is that language has "always been sexist." This is, in fact, not true. As Dale Spender (1990) notes in her book, *Man Made Language*, until 1746 when John Kirkby formulated his "Eighty Eight Grammatical Rules," the words "they" and "their" were used in sentences for sex-indeterminable sentences. Kirkby's rule number twenty-one stated that the male sex was more comprehensive than the female

and thus argued that "he" was the grammatically correct way to note men *and* women in writing where mixed sexed or sex-indeterminable situations are referred to (Spender, 1990). Women were not given equal access to education at this time and thus the male grammarians who filled the halls of the academy and had no incentive to disagree with Mr. Kirkby, accepted his eighty-eight rules in full.

Interestingly though, the general population was not as easily convinced. Perhaps because they were not used to identifying women as men in language or perhaps because it did not make rational sense to do so, the general public ignored rule number twenty-one.

Incensed by the continued misuse of "they," male grammarians were influential in the passing of the 1850 Act of Parliament which legally asserted that "he" stood for "she" (Spender, 1990). Yes, you read correctly. Parliament passed legislation in an effort to promote the use of sexist language. And it worked! Eventually the rule was adhered to by the public and thus we have the regular and rarely challenged use of sexist language. But this use of language was not "natural" or even "normal" for many millennia.

Pretending that we haven't learned about the work of Dale Spender, let's assume that language has "always been sexist." Even if language was always sexist, that does not make the use of sexist language right. We wouldn't make a similar argument about racist language, so that argument isn't any stronger with regard to language that is sexist. It simply isn't acceptable today to use sexist language; and by learning to avoid these common mistakes, you can avoid using language that is grammatically incorrect, unethical, and problematic. See Table 7-1 for examples of sexist and non-sexist language.

Is your remarkably sexist drivel intentional, or just some horrible mistake?

~ Yeardley Smith

Table 7-1 Comparison of Sexist and Gender-Neutral Terms

Sexist Terms	Gender-Neutral Terms
Actress	Actor
Ballerina	Ballet Dancer
Businessman	Business Person
Chairman	Chairperson
Fireman	Firefighter
Fisherman	Fisher
Mailman/Postman	Mail/Letter Carrier
Male Nurse	Nurse
Policeman	Police Officer
Stewardess	Flight Attendant
Waitress	Server
He (to mean men and women)	He or She, He/She, They
Example: If a student wants to do well, he must study.	Examples: If a student wants to do well, he or she must study. If students want to do well, they must study

From: http://eca.state.gov/forum/vols/vol42/no1/p36.htm#chart

First, you should avoid the use of what is called the **generic "he" or "man,"** which is the use of terms such as "mankind" instead of "humankind" or "humanity," or the use of "man" or "he" to refer to all people. A common response from students with regard to the use of "generic he" is that the word is intended to represent men *and* women, therefore when it's used it is not used to be sexist. If it were really the case that people truly recognized in their minds that the term "man" includes women, then we would talk about situations in which "man has difficulty giving birth" (Spender, 1990) or the "impact of menstruation on man's biology." Of course, we do not say those things because they simply wouldn't make sense to us. Perhaps you can now see why the people of the 1700s and 1800s had trouble switching from nonsexist to sexist language—it defied their own common sense just as discussing how "man gets pregnant" defies yours.

Second, you should avoid using **man-linked terms**, which are terms such as "fireman" or "policemen." It is appropriate to use these terms when you know that the people you are speaking about are men only, but if you do not know for sure or if you're talking about groups generally, you should avoid using these types of terms and replace them with "firefighters" and "police officers." Colleges and universities should replace "freshman" with "first-year students" and so should you. Other, non job-oriented words also suffer from this same problem. People often note that tables need to be "manned" rather than "staffed" and that items are "man-made" instead of "human made" or "handmade."

A final common use of sexist language occurs when people use **spotlighting** when discussing the occupations of men and women. How often have you heard (or used) a phrase such as "he's a male nurse" or "that female lawyer?" When we spotlight in these ways, we are pointing out that a person is deviating from the "norm" and implying that someone's sex is relevant to a particular job. According to Peccei (2003), in the English language

there is a very strong tendency to "place the adjective expressing the most 'defining' characteristic closest to the noun." Thus, as [Peccei] points out, a phrase like the "old intelligent woman" violates our sense of "correct," not because there's anything wrong with the word order grammatically, but because it contradicts our customary way of thinking that values youth over age. If you talk about a "male nurse" or a "female cop," you risk communicating to the audience that you believe the most salient aspect of a particular job is the sex of the person that *normally* does it, and some audience members may not appreciate that assumption on your part.

The use of sexist language is not just grammatically incorrect; its use is also linked to ethics because it communicates a reality that does not exist—it is *not accurate*. Man-linked language communicates male superiority and that there are more men than women because women are regularly erased linguistically in speech and writing. Man-linked terms and spotlighting communicate that some job activities are appropriate for men but not women and vice versa by putting focus on the sex of a person as linked to their job or activity. Finally, the use of the generic "he" or "man" communicates that men are the norm and women deviate from that norm. If all humans are called "man," what does that say about women? Sexist language can also limit what young males and females believe that they can accomplish in their lives. Ethical speakers should therefore avoid using language that communicates these sexist practices.

Speakers who choose to continue to use sexist language are not only speaking in a manner that is grammatically incorrect, they are also risking communicating negative ideas about themselves to audience members. Often the use of sexist language is because of a careless error, so be careful about language choice so that you don't accidentally communicate something about yourself that you didn't intend or that isn't true. Remember that if one person in your audience is offended by some aspect of your language use, they may share their opinions with others in the room. If that one person is a leader of the larger group or is someone whose opinions people care about, offending that one audience member may cause you to "lose" many other audience members as well.

Heterosexist language is language that assumes the heterosexual orientation of a person or group of people. Be careful when speaking not to use words or phrases that assume the sexual orientation of your audience members. Do not make the mistake of pointing to someone in your audience as an example and discussing that person with the assumption that she is heterosexual by saying something like, "Let's say this woman here is having trouble with her husband." When thinking of examples to use, consider using names that could ring true for heterosexuals and homosexuals alike. Instead of talking about Pat and Martha, discuss an issue involving Pat and Chris. Not only will you avoid language that assumes everyone's partner is of the opposite sex, you will also better your chances of persuading using your example. If the use of sex-specific names doesn't ring true with members of your audience that are homosexual, it is possible that they are not as likely to continue to listen to your example with the same level of interest. They are more likely to follow your example if they aren't confronted immediately with names that assume a heterosexual relationship. There are, of course, ethical considerations as well. Because it is likely that your entire audience is not heterosexual (and certainly they do not all hold heterosexist attitudes), using heterosexist language is another way that speakers may alienate audience members. In reality the world is not completely heterosexual and even in the unlikely case that you're speaking in a room of consisting completely of heterosexuals, many people have friends or relatives that are homosexual, so the use of heterosexist language to construct the world as if this were not the case runs counter to ethical communication.

Avoiding Language Pitfalls

There are other aspects of language you should consider when thinking about how language choices impact the audience's perception of you.

Profanity

It seems obvious, but this fact bears repeating—you should refrain from using profanity in your speeches. One of the primary rules of all aspects of public speaking (audience analysis, delivery, topic selection, etc.) is that you should never ignore audience expectations. Audiences do not expect speakers to use profane language, and in most cases, doing so will hurt your credibility with the audience. It is true that certain audiences will not mind an occasional profane word used for effect, but unless you are speaking to a group of people with whom you are very familiar, it is difficult to know for sure whether the majority of the audience will respond positively or negatively to such language use. If you even offend one person in an audience and that person happens to be an opinion leader for other audience members, the negative impact of your language on that one person could end up having a much larger influence on the audience's perception of you.

> *I wanted to cut down on the profanity, because I think I'm funnier without sayin' a lot of cuss words.*
> ~ **Chris Tucker**

Exaggeration

Speakers should also be careful about exaggeration. **Hyperbole** is the use of moderate exaggeration for effect and is an acceptable and useful language strategy. What is not acceptable, however, is the use of exaggeration to an extent that you risk losing credibility. For example, while it is acceptable to note that "it snows in South Texas as often as pigs fly," it would not be acceptable to state that "It never snows in South Texas." In the first case, you are using hyperbole as a form of exaggeration meant to creatively communicate an idea. In the second case, your use of exaggeration is stating something that is not true. It is unwise to use words such as "never" and "always" when speaking. It may be the case that speakers make this mistake accidentally because they are not careful with regard to word choice. We so easily throw words like "always" and "never" around in everyday conversation that this tendency transfers onto our public speeches when we are not thinking carefully about word choice.

There are two problems with the careless use of exaggeration. First, when you use words like "always" and "never," it is not likely that the statement you are making is true—as very few things *always* or *never* happen. Therefore, audiences might mistake your careless use of language for an attempt to purposefully misrepresent the truth. Second, when you suggest that something "always" or "never" happens, you are explicitly challenging your audience members to offer up evidence that contradicts your statement. Such a challenge may serve to impact your credibility negatively with the audience, as an audience member can make you look careless and/or silly by pointing out that your "always" or "never" statement is incorrect.

> *Exaggeration is a blood relation to falsehood and nearly as blamable.*
>
> **~ Hosea Ballou**

Powerless Language

Finally, think about using powerful language when speaking. Because women are more likely than men to be socialized to take the feelings of others into account, women tend to use less powerful language than men (Gamble & Gamble, 2003). Both men and women, however, can use language that communicates a lack of power. In some cases speakers use powerless language that communicates uncertainty. For example, a speaker might say "It seems to me that things are getting worse," or "In my estimation, things are getting worse." These phrases communicate a lack of certainty in your statements. It is likely that in

the case of these speeches, the speaker is arguing that some problem is getting worse, therefore more powerful language would be acceptable. Simply state that "Things are getting worse" and don't weaken your statement with phrases that communicate uncertainty.

Speakers should also beware of hedges, tag questions, and qualifiers. Examples of **hedges** would include, "I thought we should," "I sort of think," or "Maybe we should." Use more powerful statements such as "We should" or "I believe." In addition, speakers should avoid the use of **tag questions**, which are quick questions at the end of a statement that also communicate uncertainty. People who use tag questions might end a statement with "Don't you think?" or "Don't you agree?" rather than flatly stating what they believe because it can appear to audiences that you are seeking validation for your statements. **Qualifiers** such as "around" or "about" make your sentences less definitive, so generally avoid using them.

Interestingly, however, there are cases when using less powerful language may be useful. While a full discussion of these instances is out of the purview of this chapter, good speakers will recognize when they should use more or less powerful language. I tell my students that there are some cases when negotiation between two or more parties is the key and that in these instances using language that communicates complete certainty might impede fruitful negotiation because other parties may incorrectly perceive you as inflexible. On the other hand, in some cases you must "win" an argument or "beat" another speaker in order to even get to the negotiation table, and in those cases, the use of more powerful language may be warranted. It bears repeating that better speakers know how to use language in response to specific contexts in order to be successful, hence thinking about what contexts require more or less powerful language is always a good idea.

There may be times when we are powerless to prevent injustice, but there must never be a time when we fail to protest.
~ Elie Wiesel

Incorrect Grammar

While the use of sexist or heterosexist language may imply some negative qualities about you to your audience, the use of incorrect grammar in your speech will explicitly communicate negative attributes about you quite clearly. There are four primary means by which incorrect grammar tends to make its way into speeches, including basic error, mispronunciations, regionalisms, and colloquialisms.

Basic errors occur when people make simple mistakes in grammar because of carelessness or a lack of knowledge. If you are unsure about the grammatical structure of a sentence, ask someone.

Although spoken English doesn't obey the rules of written language, a person who doesn't know the rules thoroughly is at a great disadvantage.
~ Marilyn vos Savant

Practicing your speech in front of others can help you catch mistakes. Grammatical errors can also happen when speakers aren't familiar enough with their speech. If you do not know your topic well and have not given yourself an adequate amount of time for practice, you may fumble some during your speech and use incorrect grammar that you normally wouldn't use. One of the most regular critiques made of President George W. Bush is that he regularly makes grammatical errors in public. In one case President Bush stated, "Rarely is the question asked: Is our children learning?" In another instance he stated, "I have a different vision of leadership. A leadership is someone who brings people together" ("Bushisms," 2007). When President Bush makes these mistakes, many people take note and it gives his detractors ammunition to critique his ability to lead. Unlike President Bush, you do not have a team of public relations specialists ready to explain away your grammatical error so you should take great care to make sure that you're prepared to speak.

Apparently Arnold was inspired by President Bush, who proved you can be a successful politician in this country even if English is your second language.

~ Conan O'Brien

In addition, you must be sure that you are pronouncing words correctly. In one instance I had a student who began discussing the philosopher Plato, except she pronounced his name "Platt-o" instead of "Play-toe." I could see students glancing at each other and rolling their eyes in response to this mistake. Indeed, it was even difficult for me to pay attention after the mistake because it was such a blatant error. Making pronunciation mistakes, especially when you're pronouncing words that the general public deems ordinary, can seriously impede your

credibility. It was likely difficult for students to take this speaker's remaining comments seriously after she'd made such a big mistake. If you're unsure about how to pronounce a word, check with someone else or with the dictionary to make sure you're pronouncing it correctly. In fact, many online dictionaries such as Merriam-Webster.com and Dictionary. com now include a function that allows you to hear how the word is pronounced. And if it's a word you're not used to saying, such as a technical or medical term, practice saying it *out loud* 10-20 times a day until you're comfortable with the word. Remember that our mouths are machines and that our tongues, teeth, cheeks, lips, etc. all work together to pronounce sounds. When faced with a word that our mouths are not yet "trained" to say, it is more likely that we'll mispronounce the word or stutter some on it during a speech. But if you practice saying the word out loud several times a day leading up to your speech, you're less likely to make a mistake and your confidence will be boosted instead of hurt in the midst of your speech.

> *Remember: Y'all is singular. All y'all is plural. All y'all's is plural possessive.*
>
> **~ Kinky Friedman**

Some grammar problems occur because people use regionalisms when speaking, which may pose problems for people in the audience not familiar with the terms being used. **Regionalisms** are customary words or phrases used in different geographic regions. For example, growing up in Texas I used "y'all," while my students in Pennsylvania might use "youins" or "yins" to mean a group of people. In the South, many people use the phrase "Coke" to mean any soft drink (probably because Coca-Cola is headquartered in Atlanta), while in the Northeast a "Coke" might be called a "tonic" and in other regions it might be called a "pop" or "soda pop." You must be careful when using regional terms because your audience may not interpret your message correctly if they are not familiar with the regionalism you're using. Try to find terms that are broader in their use, perhaps using "you all" or "soft drink" instead of the regional terms you may be used to using in everyday conversations.

Another grammar issue often linked to region is the use of colloqui-alisms. **Colloquialisms** are words or phrases used in informal speech but not typically used in formal speech. Using the word "crick" instead of "creek" is one example of a colloquialism, and in some areas "I'm getting ready to cook dinner" would be said, "I'm fixin' to make dinner." Colloquialisms can also be phrases that stem from particular regions. In some regions nice clothes are often referred to as your "Sunday best," and in some areas, when people are preparing to vacuum, they note that they are getting ready to "red up the place" (make it ready for visitors). Like regionalisms, an audience understanding your use of colloquialisms depends on their familiarity with the language ten-dencies of a certain geographic area, so steering clear of their use can help you make sure that your message is understood by your audience. Another problem that regionalisms and colloquialisms have in com-mon is that some audience members may consider their use a sign of lesser intellect because they are not considered proper grammar, so you also risk leaving a bad impression of yourself with audience members if you make these language choices for a formal presentation.

I personally think we developed language because of our deep need to complain.

~ **Lily Tomlin**

Other Language Choices to Consider

Clichés are phrases or expressions that, because of overuse, have lost their rhetorical power. Examples include sayings such as "The early bird gets the worm" or "Making a mountain out of a molehill." Phrases such as these were once powerful ways of communicating an idea, but because of overuse these phrases just don't have the impact that they once had. Using clichés in your speeches runs the risk of having two negative attributions being placed on you by audience members. First, audience members may feel that your use of a cliché communicates that you didn't take the speech seriously and/or were lazy in construct-ing it. Second, your audience members may perceive you as someone who is not terribly creative. Clichés area easy ways to communicate your message, but you might pay for that ease with negative feelings about you as a speaker from your audience. Try to avoid using clichés so that audiences are more likely to perceive you positively as a speaker.

Another consideration for speakers is whether or not to use language central to the popular culture of a time period. Whether we're talking about "groovy, man" from the 1970s or "like totally awesome" from the 1980s, or "word to your mutha" from the 1990s, the language central to the popular culture of any time period is generally something to be avoided in formal public speaking. Like slang or profanity, language stemming from popular culture can be limited in its appeal. Some audiences may not understand it, some audiences may negatively evaluate you for using language that is too informal, and other audiences will have negative preconceived notions about "the kind of people" that use such language (e.g., "hippies" in the 1970s), and they will most likely transfer those negative evaluations onto you.

Conclusion

This chapter has discussed a number of important aspects of language that good speakers should always consider.

It is important for speakers to remember the power of language and to harness that power effectively, yet ethically. We've discussed the relationship between the language we use and the way we see the world, the importance of using language that is clear, vivid, stylized, ethical and that reflects well on you as the speaker. The difference between choosing one word over another can be as significant as an audience member remembering your presentation or forgetting it and/

or an audience turning against you and your ideas. Taking a few extra moments to add some alliteration or to check for language that might offend others is time very well spent. The next time you have to write or speak about an issue, remember the importance of language and its impact on our lives— carefully consider what language will you use and how will those language choices make a difference in how your audiences defines and understands your topic.

> *If you talk to a man in a language he understands, that goes to his head. If you talk to him in his language, that goes to his heart.*
>
> ~ **Nelson Mandela**

Glossary

Alliteration
The repetition of the initial sounds of words.
Antithesis
Rhetorical strategy that uses contrasting statements in order to make a rhetorical point.
Clichés
Phrases or expressions that, because of overuse, have lost their rhetorical power.
Colloquialisms
Words or phrases used in informal speech but not typically used in formal speech.
Communication
Attempts to reproduce what is in our minds in the minds of our audience.
Generic "he" or "man"
Language that uses words such as "he" or "mankind" to refer to the male *and* female population.
Hedges

Powerless phrases such as "I thought we should," "I sort of think," or "Maybe we should" that communicate uncertainty.

Heterosexist Language

Language that assumes the heterosexual orientation of a person or group of people.

Hyperbole

The use of moderate exaggeration for effect.

Jargon

The specialized language of a group or profession.

Language

The means by which we communicate—a system of symbols we use to form messages.

Man-linked Terms

Terms such as "fireman" or "policemen" that incorrectly identify a job as linked only to a male.

Metaphors

Comparisons made by speaking of one thing in terms of another.

Qualifiers

Powerless words such as "around" or "about" that make your sentences less definitive.

Regionalisms

Customary words or phrases used in different geographic regions.

Sexist Language

Language that unnecessarily identifies sex or linguistically erases females through the use of man-linked terms and/or the use of "he" or "man" as generics.

Similes

Comparisons made by speaking of one thing in terms of another using the word "like" or "as" to make the comparison.

Slang

Type of language that most people understand but that is not considered acceptable in formal or polite conversation.

Spotlighting

Language such as "male nurse" that suggests a person is deviating from the "normal" person who would do a particular job and implies that someone's sex is relevant to a particular job.

Tag Questions
Powerless language exemplified by ending statements with questions such as "Don't you think?" or "Don't you agree?"

References

Bushisms—U.S. President proves how difficult English really is! (2011). Retrieved from http://esl.about.com/library/weekly/aa032301a.htm

Gamble, T. K. & Gamble, M. W. (2003). *The gender communication connection*. New York, NY: Houghton-Mifflin.

Haigledygook and secretaryspeak. (1981, February 23). Retrieved from http://www.time.com/time/magazine/article/0,9171,949069,00.html

Hamilton, G. (2008). *Public speaking for college and career* (8th ed.). New York, NY: McGraw-Hill.

Jackson, J. (1984). 1984 Democratic National Convention address. Retrieved from http://www.americanrhetoric.com/speeches/jessejackson198 4dnc.htm

King, M. L., Jr. (1963). I have a dream. Retrieved from http://www.americanrhetoric.com/speeches/mlkihaveadream.htm

Peccei, J. S. (2003). Language and age. In I. Singh & J. S. Peccei (Eds.), *Language, society, and power: An introduction* (2nd ed.). New York, NY: Routledge.

Spender, D. (1990). *Man made language*. New York, NY: Pandora.

Photo Credits

Rail Forum by Michigan Municipal League
http://www.flickr.com/photos/michigancommunities/5041931910/

Rev. Martin Luther King Jr. by Dick DeMarcisco
http://commons.wikimedia.org/wiki/File:Martin_Luther_King_Jr_NY-WTS_6.jpg

Secretary of State Alexander Haig by University of Texas
http://commons.wikimedia.org/wiki/File:Al_Haig_speaks_to_
press_1981.jpg
LAMB Teal Wrap Sweater
http://www.bluefly.com/
Goth people by Rama
http://commons.wikimedia.org/wiki/File:Goth_f222791.jpg
Audience at Next conference by NEXT Berlin
http://www.flickr.com/photos/nextconference/4633552536/
"Feminazi" coined by Rush Limbaugh, see
http://www.merriam-webster.com/dictionary/feminazi
Italian Soldier by the Italian Army
http://commons.wikimedia.org/wiki/File:Italian_Soldier_Olypmic_
Games_Turin_2006.jpg
Married gay couple by John
http://commons.wikimedia.org/wiki/File:Married_Gay_Couple_John_
and_Jamie.jpg
Malalai Joya by AfghanKabul
http://www.flickr.com/photos/19712640@N05/2076699646/
Dilgo Khyentse Yangsi Rinpoche by Wonderlane
http://www.flickr.com/photos/wonderlane/4915821372/

Public Narrative, Collective Action, and Power

By Marshall Ganz

The authors of [related chapters] ask how discontented, but compliant, publics can mobilize to demand political change. It is not obvious. Organized collective action to challenge the status quo, as opposed to the occasional outburst of resentment, does not "just happen." Nor does it occur as an automatic response to the availability of tools described elsewhere—citizen report cards, public expenditure tracking, participatory budgeting, social audits, right-to-information acts, and so on. Nor does it arise as a result of a providential convergence of resources and opportunities, as often described by social movement theorists.

Organized collective action challenging the status quo—a social movement— requires leadership that goes far beyond a stereotypical charismatic public persona with whom it is often identified. Unable to rely on established bureaucratic structures for coordination, evaluation, and action, such action depends on voluntary participation, shared commitments, and ongoing motivation. Movements must mobilize under risky conditions not only because well- resourced oppositions often resist their efforts, but also because the undertaking itself is fraught with uncertainty about how—and whether—it can happen in the first place. The capacity of a social movement for effective action

Marshall Ganz; eds. Sina Odugbemi and Taeku Lee, "Public Narrative, Collective Action, and Power," Accountability Through Public Opinion: From Inertia to Public Action, pp. 273-289. Copyright © 2011 by The World Bank Group. Reprinted with permission.

Figure 8-1   Mobilization of Others

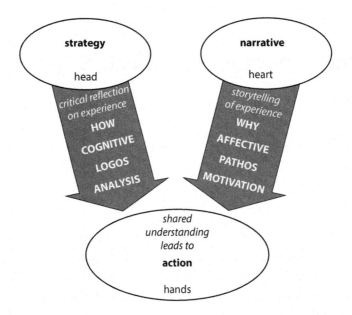

Zac Willette and the author

depends largely on the depth, breadth, and quality of leadership able to turn opportunity to purpose.

Mobilizing others to achieve purpose under conditions of uncertainty—what leaders do—challenges the hands, the head, and the heart. As shown in figure 8-1, the challenge of the "hands" is one of action, of learning, of adapting, and of mastering novel skills. The challenge of the head is one of strategy, imagining how to transform one's resources into the power needed to achieve one's purpose. The challenge of the heart is one of motivation, of urgent need to act, and of hope for success, and the courage to risk it. This is the work of public narrative, the focus of this chapter.

Public narrative is a leadership practice of translating values into action. It is based on the fact that values are experienced emotionally. As such, they are sources of ends worthy of action and the capacity for action. Narrative is the discursive means we use to access values that equip us with the courage to make choices under conditions

Figure 8-3 Motivating Action

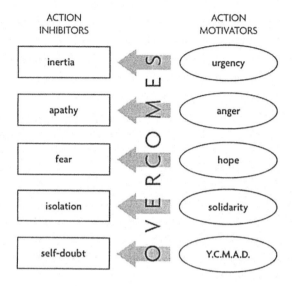

Note: Y.C.M.A.D. = You Can Make A Difference.

Zac Willette and the author

We can counter *inertia* with *urgency*. Urgency can capture our attention, creating the space for new action. But it is less about time than about priority. My need to complete a problem set due tomorrow supplants a more important need to figure out what to do with the rest of life. An urgent need to attend to a critically ill family member supplants an important need to attend the next business meeting.

Commitment and concentration of energy are required to launch anything new, and creating a sense of urgency often is a critical way to get the commitment that is required. Imagine that someone calls you and says that he is recruiting for a 100-year plan to change the world. This is the beginning, and he will call a meeting sometime over the next six months. Would you be interested in going to that meeting, whenever it happens? However, what if someone calls about an election you care about, with news that the campaign has to contact 3,000 targeted voters before Election Day, just one week away?

This person tells you that if 220 volunteers contact 20 voters each, they can reach all the voters and bring this election home— that if you come to the headquarters at 6:00 tonight, you will meet the other volunteers and learn how to reach 20 key voters in your neighborhood. Are you interested? Urgency recognizes that "time is like an arrow." Because launching anything new requires commitment and intense effort, urgency is often the way to make it happen.

What about inertia's first cousin, *apathy*? One way to counter apathy is with *anger*—not rage, but outrage or indignation with injustice. Anger often grows out of experience of a contrast between *the world as it is* and *the world as it ought to be*, how we feel when our moral order has been violated (Alinsky, 1971). Sociologist Bill Gamson (1992) describes this as using an "injustice frame" to counter a "legitimacy frame." As scholars of "moral economy" have taught us, people rarely mobilize to protest inequality as such, but they do mobilize to protest "unjust" inequality (Scott, 1976). In other words, our values, moral traditions, and sense of personal dignity function as critical sources of the motivation to act. This is one reason that organizing is so deeply rooted in moral traditions.

Where can we find the *courage* to act in spite of our *fear*? Trying to eliminate that to which we react fearfully is a fool's errand because it locates the source of our fear outside ourselves, rather than within our hearts. However, trying to make ourselves "fearless" is counterproductive if we wind up acting more out of "nerve than brain." Leaders sometimes prepare others for fear by warning them that the opposition will threaten them with this and woo them with that. The fact that these behaviors are expected reveals the opposition as more predictable and, thus, less to be feared.

What can we do about fear? A choice to act in spite of fear is the meaning of courage. Of all the emotions that help us find courage, perhaps most important is *hope*. So where do you go to get some hope? One source of hope is experience of a "credible solution," not only reports of success elsewhere, but also direct experience of small successes and small victories. A source of hope for many people is in their faith tradition, grounded in spiritual beliefs, cultural traditions, and moral understandings. Many of the great social movements— Gandhi, civil rights, and Solidarity—drew strength from religious traditions, and much of today's organizing is grounded in faith communities.

Relationships offer another source of hope. We all know people who inspire hopefulness just by being around them. "Charisma" can be seen as the capacity to inspire hope in others, inspiring others to believe in themselves. Many people have charisma, but some of us need to be encouraged to use it. Just as religious belief requires a "leap of faith," Cornel West (1994) argues that politics requires a "leap of hope." More philosophically, Moses Maimonides, the Jewish scholar of the 15th century, argued that hope is belief in the "plausibility of the possible" as opposed to the "necessity of the probable." And psychologists who explore the role of "positive emotions" give particular attention to the "psychology of hope" (Seligman & Csikszentmihali, 2000). In concert with *confidence* and *solidarity*, hope can move us to act.

We can counter feelings of *isolation* with the experience of *belovedness* or *solidarity*. This is the role of mass meetings, singing, common dress, and shared language. This is why developing relationships with the people whom we hope to mobilize is important. Because of the snowball effect, it is much easier to get people to join others who are already active.

Finally, one of the biggest inhibitors is *self-doubt:* I cannot do it. People like me cannot do it. We are not qualified, and so on. When we feel *isolated,* we fail to appreciate the interests we share with others, we are unable to access our common resources, we have no sense of a shared identity, and we feel powerless. We can counter self-doubt with *YCMAD: You Can Make A Difference.* The best way to inspire this belief is to frame what you do around *what people can do,* not what they cannot do. If you design a plan calling for each new volunteer to recruit 100 people, and you provide no leads, training, or coaching, you will only create deeper feelings of self-doubt. It is also important to recognize specific people for specific contributions at specific times and in specific ways. Recognition must be based on real accomplishment, however, not empty flattery. The idea is to spread accomplishment around and then recognize people for those accomplishments. There is no recognition without personal *accountability.* Requiring accountability does not show lack of trust, but is evidence that what one is doing really matters. Have you ever volunteered to walk a precinct in a campaign? You are given a packet with a voter list and told to mark the responses on the list and to bring it back when you are done. What happens if you go out for four hours, do a conscientious job, and return to headquarters ready to report, only to hear, "Oh, thanks a lot. Just throw it over there in the corner. See you next week." What about all your work? Did it not matter enough for anyone to debrief you about it, let alone mark it on a wall chart and try to learn from it? Do you think you will go back "next week?"

Telling Your Public Story

Storytelling is the discursive form through which we translate our values into the motivation to act. As shown in figure 8-4, a story is crafted of just three elements: *plot, character,* and *moral.* The effect depends on the *setting:* who tells the story, who listens, where they are, why they are there, and when.

Plot

A plot engages us, captures our interest, and makes us pay attention. "I got up this morning, had breakfast, and came to school." Is that a plot? Why? Why not?

How about the following: "I was having breakfast this morning when I heard a loud screeching coming from the roof. At that very moment, I looked outside to where my car was parked, but it was gone!" Now what is going on? What is the difference?

A story begins. An actor is moving toward a desired goal. Then some kind of challenge appears. The plan is suddenly up in the air. The actor must figure out what to do. This is when we get interested. We want to find out what happens.

Why do we care?

Figure 8-4   Elements of a Story

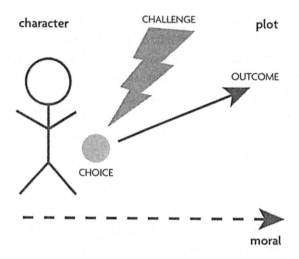

Narrative Structure

Zac Willette and the author

Dealing with the unexpected—small and large—defines the texture of our lives. No more tickets at the movie theater. You are about to lose your job. Our marriage is on the verge of break-up. We are constantly faced with the unexpected, and what we are going to do. What is the source of the greatest uncertainty around us? Other people. The subject of most stories is about how to interact with other people.

As human beings, we make choices in the present, based on re-membering the past and imagining the future. This is what it means to be an *agent.* When we act out of habit, however, we do not choose; we just follow the routine. It is only when the routines break down, when the guidelines are unclear, when no one can tell us what to do, that we make real choices and become the creators of our own lives, communities, and futures. Then we become the agents of our own fate. These moments can be as frightening as they are exhilarating.

A plot consists of just three elements: a *challenge,* a *choice,* and an *outcome.* Attending to a plot is how we learn to deal with the unpredictable. Researchers report that most of the time that parents spend with their children is in storytelling—stories of the family, the child's stories, stories of the neighbors. Bruner (1986) describes this as *agency training:* the way we learn how to process choices in the face of uncertainty. Because our curiosity about the unexpected is infinite, we invest billions of dollars and countless hours in films, literature, and sports events, not to mention religious practices, cultural activities, and national celebrations.

Character

Although a story requires a plot, it works only if we can identify with a character. Through our empathetic identification with a protagonist, we experience the emotional content of the story. That is how we learn what the story has to teach our hearts, not only our heads. As Aristode wrote of Greek tragedy in *The Poetics,* this is how the protagonist's experience can touch us and, perhaps, open our eyes. Arguments persuade with evidence, logic, and data. Stories persuade by this empathetic identification. Have you ever been to a movie where you could not identify with any of the characters? You found it boring. Sometimes we identify with protagonists who are only vaguely "like us"—like the road runner (if not the coyote) in the cartoons. Other times, we identify with protagonists who are very much like us—as in stories about friends, relatives, neighbors. Sometimes the protagonists of a story are *us,* as when we find ourselves in the midst of an unfolding story in which we are the authors of the outcome.

Moral

Stories teach. We have all heard the ending "and that is the moral of the story." Have you ever been at a party where someone starts telling a story and goes on ... and on ... and on ... ? Someone may say (or want to say), "Get to the point!" We deploy stories to *make a point* and to evoke a response.

The moral of a successful story is felt understanding, not simply conceptual understanding. When stated only conceptually, many a moral becomes a banality. We do not retell the story of David and Goliath because it teaches us how to vanquish giants. What the story teaches is that a "little guy"—with courage, resourcefulness, and imagination—can beat a "big guy," especially one with Goliath's arrogance. A fearful character, out of anger, acts courageously and emerges victorious. We feel David's fear, anger, and courage, and we feel *hopeful* for our own lives because he is victorious. Stories thus teach how to manage our emotions when challenged—how to be courageous, keep our cool, and trust our imagination— rather than the specific tactics to use in any one case.

Stories teach us how to act in the "right" way. They are not simply examples and illustrations. When stories are well told, we experience *the point*, and we feel hope. It is that experience, not the words as such, that can move us to action, because sometimes that is the point—we have to act.

Setting

Stories are told. They are not a disembodied string of words, images, and phrases. They are not messages, sound bites, or brands, although these rhetorical fragments may reference a story. Storytelling is fundamentally relational.

As we listen, we evaluate the story, and we find it more or less easy to enter, depending on the storyteller. Is it his or her story? We hear it one way. Is it the story of a friend, a colleague, or a family member? We hear it another way. Is it a story without time, place, or specificity? We step back. Is it a story we share, perhaps a Bible story? Perhaps we draw closer to one another. Storytelling is how we interact with each other about values—how we share experiences with each other, counsel each other, comfort each other, and inspire each other to action.

Public Narrative:
Story of Self—Story of Us—Story of Now

Leadership, especially leadership on behalf of social change, often requires telling a new public story, or adapting an old one: a story of self, a story of us, and a story of now. As shown in figure 8-5, story of self communicates the values that move us to lead. A story of us communicates values shared by those whom you hope to motivate to join us. And a story of now communicates the urgent challenge to those values that demands action now. Participating in a social action not only often involves a rearticulating of one's story of self, us, and now, but also marks an entry into a world of uncertainty so daunting that access to sources of hope is essential. To illustrate, I'll draw examples from the first seven minutes of then Senator Barack Obama's speech to the Democratic National Convention in July 2004.

Figure 8-5   Self, Us, Now

Public Narrative

Zac Willette and the author

Story of Self

Telling one's Story of Self is a way to share the values that define who you are—not as abstract principles, but as lived experience. We construct stories of self around *choice points*—moments when we faced a challenge, made a choice, experienced an outcome, and learned a moral. We communicate values that motivate us by selecting from among those choice points, and recounting what happened. Because storytelling is a social transaction, we engage our listener's memories as well as our own as we learn to adapt our story of self in response to feedback so the communication is successful. Similarly, like the response to the Yiddish riddle that asks who discovered water—"I don't know, but it wasn't a fish"—the other person often can "connect the dots" that we may not have connected because we are so within our own story that we have not learned to articulate them.

We construct our identity, in other words, as our story. What is utterly unique about each of us is not a combination of the categories (race, gender, class, profession, and marital status) that include us, but rather, our journey, our way through life, our personal text from which each of us can teach (Hammack, 2008).

A story is like a poem. A poem moves not by how long it is, nor by how eloquent or complicated. A story or poem moves by evoking an experience or moment through which we grasp the feeling or insight the poet communicates. Because we are gifted with episodic memory, based on our ability to visualize past experience, we can imagine ourselves in the scene described (Tulving, 2002). The more specific the details we choose to recount, the more we can move our listeners, the more powerfully we can articulate our values, what moral philosopher Charles Taylor (1989) calls our "moral sources." Like a poem, a story can open a portal to the transcendent. Telling *about* a story is different from telling a story. When we tell a story, we enable the listener to enter its time and place with us, see what we see, hear what we hear, feel what we feel. An actor friend once told me the key was to speak entirely in the present tense and avoid using the word "and": I step into the room. It is dark. I hear a sound. Etc.

Some of us may think our personal stories don't matter, that others won't care or that we should not talk about ourselves so much. On the contrary, if we do public work we have a responsibility to give a public account of ourselves: where we came from, why we do what we do, and where we think we're going. In a role of public leadership, we really don't have a choice about telling our story of self. If we don't author our story, others will. And they may tell our story in ways that we may not like, not because they are malevolent, but because others try to make sense of who we are by drawing on their experience of people whom they consider to be like us. Aristotle argued that rhetoric has three components—*logos,* pathos, and *ethos*—and this is ethos. The logos is the logic of the argument. The pathos is the feeling the argument evokes. The ethos is the credibility of the person who makes the argument—his or her story of self.

Social movements are often the "crucibles" within which participants learn to tell new stories of self as we interact with other participants. Stories of self can be challenging because participation in social change is often prompted by a "prophetic" combination of criticality and hope. In personal terms, this means that most participants have stories of both the world's pain and the world's hope. And if we haven't talked about our stories of pain very much, it can take a while to learn to manage it. But if others try to make sense of why we are doing what we are doing and we leave this piece out, our account will lack authenticity, raising questions about the rest of the story.

In the early days of the women's movement, people participated in "consciousness raising" group conversations that mediated changes in their stories of self, who they were, as a woman. Stories of pain could be shared, but so could stories of hope (Polletta, 2006). In the civil rights movement, blacks living in the Deep South who feared claiming the right to vote had to encourage one another to find the courage to make the claim, which, once made, began to alter how they thought of themselves and how they could interact with their children, as well as with white people, and each other (Cuoto, 1993).

In Senator Obama's "story of self," he recounts three key choice points: his grandfather's decision to send his son to America to study;

his parents' "improbable" decision to marry; and his parents' decision to name him Barack ("blessing"), an expression of faith in a tolerant and generous America. He also references his grandfather's choice to enlist and serve in "Patton's army" and his grandmother's choice to "work on a bomber assembly line AND raise a family." Each choice communicates courage, hope, and caring. He tells us nothing of his resumé, preferring to introduce himself by telling us where he came from, and who made him the person that he is, so that we might have an idea of where he is going.

Story of Us

A public story is not only an account of the speaker's personal experience. All self stories are "nested," including fragments of other stories drawn from our culture, our faith, our parents, our friends, the movies we have seen, and the books we have read. Although individuals have their own stories, communities, movements, organizations, and nations weave collective stories out of distinct threads. Our individual threads intersected on the day that John F. Kennedy was assassinated or the day we saw the planes hit the Twin Towers. We shared a crisis, and we learned the morals about how we are to act and how life is to be lived. Points of intersection become the focus of a shared story—the way we link individual threads into a common weave. A Story of Us brings forward the values that move us as a community.

How does the storyteller become part of this larger story? Learning to tell a story of us requires deciding who the "us" is—which values shape that identity and which are most relevant to the situation at hand. Stories then not only teach us how to live, but also teach us how to distinguish who "we" are from "others," reducing uncertainty about what to expect from our community. In the midst of treacherous weather, earthquakes, disease, and other environmental sources of great unpredictability, the behavior, actions, and reactions of the people among whom we live, and our shared stock of stories, give us greater safety.

Our cultures are repositories of stories. Community stories about challenges we have faced, why we stood up to them—our values and our shared goals—and how we overcame them are woven throughout our political beliefs and religious traditions. We tell community stories again and again as folk sayings, popular songs, religious rituals, and community celebrations (for example, Easter, Passover, and the 4th of July). Just like individual stories, collective stories can inspire hope or generate despair. We also weave new stories from old ones. The Exodus story, for example, served the Puritans when they colonized North America, but it also served Southern blacks claiming their civil rights in the freedom movement (MacIntyre, 2001).

Organizations that lack a "story" lack an identity, a culture, core values that can be articulated and drawn on to motivate. Leaders learn to tell the story of us—the story of their organization—by identifying the "choice points" of the organization's journey, recounting experiences that communicate the values embedded in the work of the organization.

As figure 8-5 shows, our stories of self overlap with our stories of us. We participate in many us's: family, community, faith, organization, profession, nation, or movement. A story of us expresses the values, the experiences, shared by the us we hope to evoke at the time. A story of "us" not only articulates the values of our community, but also can distinguish our community from another, thus reducing uncertainty about what to expect from those with whom we interact. Social scientists often describe a "story of us" as a collective identity (Somers, 1992, 1994).

For a collection of people to become an "us" requires a storyteller, an interpreter of shared experience. In a workplace, for example, people who work beside one another but interact little, don't linger after work, don't arrive early, and don't eat together never develop a story of us. In a social movement, the interpretation of the movement's new experience is a critical leadership function. And, like the story of self, it is built from the choice points—the founding, the choices made, the challenges faced, the outcomes, and the lessons it learned.

In Senator Obama's speech, he moves into his "story of us" when he declares, "My story is part of the American story," and proceeds to list values he shares with his listeners—the people in the room, the people watching on television, the people who will read about it the next day. And he begins by going back to the beginning, to choices made by the founders to begin this nation, a beginning that he locates in the Declaration of Independence—a repository of the value of equality.

Story of Now

Stories of Now articulate the challenges we face now, the choices we are called upon to make, and the meaning of making the right choice. Stories of Now are set in the past, present, and future. The challenge is now; we are called on to act because of our legacy and who we have become, and the action that we take now can shape our desired future.

These are stories in which we are the protagonists. We face a crisis, a challenge. It is our choice to make. We have a story of hope, if we make the right choice. The storyteller among us whom we have authorized to "narrativize" this moment finds a way to articulate our crisis and challenge as a choice, reminds us of our moral resources (our stories—stories of our family, our community, our culture, and our faith), and offers a hopeful vision we can share as we take our first steps on the journey.

A story of now articulates an urgent challenge—or threat—to the values that we share that demands action now. What choice must we make? What is at risk? And where's the hope? In a story of now, we are the protagonists and it is our choices that shape the outcome. We draw on our "moral sources" to find the courage, hope, empathy perhaps to respond. A most powerful articulation of a story of now was Dr. Martin Luther King's speech delivered in Washington, D.C., on August 23, 1963, often recalled as the "I Have a Dream" speech. People often forget that what preceded the dream was a nightmare: the consequence of white America's failure to make good on its promissory note to African Americans. King (1963) argued the moment was possessed of the "fierce urgency of now" because this debt could no longer be postponed. If we did not act, the nightmare would only grow worse—for all of us—never to become the dream.

In a story of now, story and strategy overlap because a key element in hope is a strategy—a credible vision of *how to get from here to there*. The "choice" offered cannot be something such as "we must all choose to be better people" or "we must all choose to do any one of this list of 53 things" (which makes each of them trivial). A meaningful choice is more like "we all must choose: Do we commit to boycotting the busses until they desegregate or not?" Hope is specific, not abstract. What's the vision? When God inspires the Israelites in Exodus 3:9, he doesn't offer a vague hope of "better days," but describes a land "flowing with milk and honey" and what must be done to get there. A vision of hope can unfold a chapter at a time. It can begin by getting that number of people to show up at a meeting that you committed to do. You can win a "small" victory that shows change is possible. A small victory can become a source of hope if it is *interpreted* as part of a greater vision. In churches, when people have a "new story" to tell about themselves, it is often in the form of "testimony"—a person sharing an account of moving from despair to hope, the significance of the experience strengthened by the telling of it. Hope is not to be found in lying about the facts, but in the *meaning* we give to the facts. Shakespeare's "King Henry V" stirs hope in his men's hearts by offering them a different view of themselves. No longer are they a few bedraggled soldiers led by a young and inexperienced king in an obscure corner of France who is about to be wiped out by an overwhelming force. Now they are a "happy few," united with their king in solidarity, holding an opportunity to grasp immortality in their hands, to become legends in their own time—a legacy for their children and grand children (Shakespeare, Henry V, Act IV, Scene 3). This is their time! The story of now is that moment in which story (why) and strategy (how) overlap and in which, as poet Seamus Heaney (1991) writes, "Justice can rise up, and hope and history rhyme." And for the claim to be credible, the action must begin right here, right now, in this room, with action each one of us can take. It's the story of a credible strategy, with an account of how, starting with who and where we are, and how we can, step-by-step, get to where we want to go. Our action can call forth the actions of others, and their actions can call others, and together these actions can carry the day. It's like Pete Seeger's old protest song, "One Man's Hands," which reminds us that the targets of social change—from prison walls to unaccountable governments—cannot fall at the hands of any one person, but rather require the concerted hands of a collectivity.

Senator Obama moves to his "story of now" with the phrase, "There is more work left to do." After we have shared in the experience of values we identify with America at its best, he confronts us with the fact that they are not realized in practice. He then tells stories of specific people in specific places with specific problems. As we identify with each of them, our empathy reminds us of pain we have felt in our own lives. But, he also reminds us, all this could change. And we know it could change. And it could change because we have a way to make the change, if we choose to take it. And that way is to support the election of Senator John Kerry. Although that last part didn't work out, the point is that he concluded his story of now with a very specific choice he calls upon us to make.

Through public narrative, leaders—and participants—can move to action by mobilizing sources of motivation, constructing new shared individual and collective identities, and finding the courage to act.

Celebrations

We do much of our storytelling in celebrations. A celebration is not a party. It is a way that members of a community come together to honor who they are, what they have done, and where they are going—often symbolically. Celebrations may occur at times of sadness, as well as times of great joy. Celebrations provide rituals that allow us to join in enacting a vision of our community—at least in our hearts. Institutions that retain their vitality are rich in celebrations. In the Church, for example, Mass is "celebrated." Harvard's annual celebration is called Graduation and lasts an entire week.

Storytelling is at its most powerful at beginnings—for individuals, their childhood; for groups, their formation; for movements, their launching; and for nations, their founding. Celebrations are a way we interpret important events, recognize important contributions, acknowledge a common identity, and deepen our sense of community. The way that we interpret these moments begins to establish norms, create expectations, and shape patterns of behavior, which then influence all subsequent development. We draw on them again and again. Nations institutionalize their founding story as a renewable source of guidance and inspiration. Most faith traditions enact a weekly retelling of their story of redemption, usually rooted in their founding. Well-told stories help turn moments of great crises into moments of "new beginnings."

Conclusion

Narrative allows us to communicate the emotional content of our values. Narrative is not talking "about" values; rather, narrative embodies and communicates those values. It is through the shared experience of our values that we can engage with others; motivate one another to act; and find the courage to take risks, explore possibility, and face the challenges we must face. Public narrative, understood as a leadership art, is thus an invaluable resource to stem the tides of apathy, alienation, cynicism, and defeatism. Stories, strategically told, can powerfully rouse a sense of urgency; hope; anger; solidarity; and the belief that individuals, acting in concert, can make a difference.

References

Alinsky, S. (1971). *Rules for radicals.* New York, NY: Random House.

Bruner, J. (1986). Two Modes of Thought. In *Actual minds, possible worlds.* Cambridge, MA: Harvard University Press.

Cuoto, R. A. (1993). Narrative, free space, and political leadership in social movements. *Journal of Politics, 55,* 57–79.

Gamson, W. A. (1992). *Talking politics.* New York, NY: Cambridge University Press.

Hammack, P. L. (2008). Narrative and the cultural psychology of identity. *Personality and Social Psychology Review 12,* 222–47.

Heaney, S. (1991). *The cure at Troy: A version of Sophocles'* Philoctetes. New York, NY: Farrar, Straus, and Giroux.

King, M. L., Jr. (1963) I have a dream. Retrieved from http://www.american-rhetoric.com/speeches/mlkihaveadream.htm.

MacIntyre, A. (2001). The virtues, the unity of a human life, and the concept of a tradition. In L. P. Hinchman & S. K. Hinchman (Eds.), *Memory, identity, community: The idea of narrative in the human sciences.* Albany, NY: State University of New York Press.

Marcus, G. E. (2002). *The sentimental citizen: Emotion in democratic politics.* University Park, PA: Penn State University Press.

Nussbaum, M. (2001). *Upheavals of thought: The intelligence of emotions.* New York, NY: Cambridge University Press.

Polletta, F. (2006). *It was like a fever: Storytelling in protest and politics.* Chicago, IL: University of Chicago Press.

Sayings of the Jewish fathers (Pirqe Aboth). (n.d.). Retrieved from http://www.sacred-texts.com/jud/sjf/

Scott, J. C. (1976). *The moral economy of the peasant.* New Haven, CT: Yale University Press.

Seligman, M. E. P., & Csikszentmihali, M. (2000). Positive psychology: An introduction. *American Psychologist, 55,* 5–14.

Shakespeare, W. (n.d.). *Henry V.* Retrieved from http://shakespeare.mit.edu/henryv/index.html

Somers, M. (1992). Narrativity, narrative identity, and social action: Rethinking English working-class formation. *Social Science History, 16,* 591–629.

Somers, M. (1994). The narrative constitution of identity: A relational and network approach. *Theory and Society*, 23, 605–649.

Saint Augustine. (1991). *Confessions* (H. Chadwick, Trans.). New York, NY: Oxford University Press.

Taylor, C. (1989). *Sources of the self: The making of the modern identity*. Cambridge, MA: Harvard University Press.

Tulving, E. (2002). Episodic memory: From mind to brain. *Annual Review of Psychology*, 53, 1–25.

West, C. (1994). *Race matters*. New York, NY: Vintage Books.

Topic Development/Informative Speaking

By Laura Arnett Smith

You will now begin the speech-making process introduced [ear-lier] to begin working on your informative speech. To do this, you must first choose a broad topic, then narrow the topic and write a specific-purpose statement. As you continue through this [chapter], use the models below to refer to the stages of this process. You will do

Laura Arnett Smith, "Topic Development/Informative Speaking," Leading Your Audience: A Systematic Approach to Public Speaking, pp. 45-54. Copyright © 2012 by Cognella, Inc. Reprinted with permission.

this again for your persuasive speech. Notice that you will begin the process with a broad topic and become more specific as it develops.

Selecting a Topic

The first step in the speech-making process is selecting the broad subject of the speech. Generally, this step is thought of as topic selection.

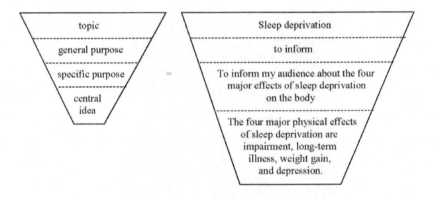

There is no such thing as the "perfect topic." Thus, try not to dwell on your decision to the point that you are not using your time wisely or that you become indecisive.

Your success with this step depends on how you approach the topic. Select a topic that you find interesting and/or feel strongly about. Avoid trivial topics. Instead, choose a topic that is worth hearing about and has value for both you and the audience. When your goal is to inform, choose a topic relevant to your audience. Think about what your audience needs to learn. When speaking to persuade, choose a topic that you care about that involves more than one viewpoint. When considering a speech topic, begin brainstorming for ideas using the following criteria:

- **Topics that you know.** Draw upon your personal experiences when you begin the brainstorming process to select a topic. You know more than you think you do. You have a wealth of experiences that others do not possess. Consider topics that will allow you to build on your current knowledge of the topic. Do not, however, choose a familiar topic because you think it will be less work. You will find that no matter how much knowledge you have on a topic, you will do the same amount of research since, as a speaker, you are not a source. In fact, most students who select a topic about which they are knowledgeable are presented with an additional challenge. When you know a great deal about a subject, it is often difficult to relate to others with little or no knowledge of the topic. Students familiar with a topic tend to deliver speeches with too much technical information for the less experienced listener.
- **Topics that interest you.** You may want to consider choosing a topic that you are interested in and want to learn more about. Since you will be spending a considerable amount of time and energy researching and preparing your speech regardless, why not use the time to learn about something new and fascinating? Your interest in this type of topic may be sparked by a news report or by what you observe on a day-to-day basis in others' conversations. Use this opportunity to expand your knowledge.
- **Topics that you care about.** Each of us cares about issues, people, places, and ideas. Consider what you feel strongly enough about that warrants sharing with your audience. This should be the case, especially in selecting a persuasive topic. If you do not care about what you are asking them to believe or do, it will make the process more tedious for you and make it obvious to your audience that the content is not very important to you.

You will probably find that many of the topics generated from this brainstorming activity you are asked to do will overlap. While this may occur, it is important to continue brainstorming until you have generated at least twelve separate topics (three for each category) without overlap. In addition, do Internet research for ideas. From these, consider which topic you can more realistically turn into an informative or persuasive speech.

General Purpose

The **general purpose** is the broad-based goal of a speech, and is usually made clear to the speaker when he or she is invited or assigned to deliver a speech. The five general purposes of a speech are to inform the audience, to persuade the audience, to entertain the audience, to inspire the audience, or to introduce someone to the audience. The first two are considered scholarly speeches, while the last three are types of special-occasion speeches. Keep in mind that speakers are often confronted with situations in which they must pursue more than one general objective at a time. For example, when delivering a persuasive speech to an audience with little or no knowledge of the topic, the speaker will find it necessary to inform the audience about the topic as well as persuade them to accept a particular viewpoint.

Specific Purpose

The **specific purpose** is a single phrase that focuses on only one aspect of your topic. It should state precisely what you hope to accomplish in the speech. The more specific the purpose, the easier it is to measure. Moreover, the specific-purpose statement is useful because it forces you to zero in on one aspect of your broad topic. You will not have time in short, classroom speeches to talk about more than one aspect of your topic. This is difficult for many speakers because, if you already know a lot about the topic or you have found a great deal of information while researching, you will want to talk about everything you know or found. This is why you should focus more time narrowing your topic than choosing the topic itself.

You must always write a specific purpose before you begin preparing your speech. This is essential because both your preparation and delivery must be focused on achieving that specific purpose. If your specific purpose is not clear, you have no comprehensible guide for how to research, organize, or prepare in general. Use the following example/formula of a specific purpose to write your own.

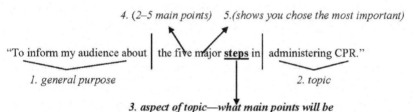

1. It always begins with the general purpose: "To inform my audience about," "to persuade my audience to," "to entertain my audience by," "to introduce my audience to," or "to inspire my audience by."
2. The broad topic should always be at the end.
3. This word tells what the main points will become. All of your main points will be the same type of thing. As you narrow the focus of the topic to one aspect, you will need to decide on the word that will best accomplish this goal. Some examples of this word can include: causes, stages, procedures, effects, ways, types, criteria, purposes, techniques, eras, steps, and so on. You cannot continue to write a central idea until you have this word.

4. For a speech of this length for class, you will have time for only two to five main points. You will not know how many main points there will be until the research is complete. Until you are definite about this number, write "two to five" each time you write a specific purpose. You can go back to "plug in" a number later in the process.

5. The word "major" signifies that there are more than five main points and you have chosen to discuss either the two to five most important, or you have combined main points together into two to five. For example, there may be thirteen separate steps to administering CPR. In this case, the speaker should combine the steps and place them into a few broad categories. The first three steps would be combined to create one main point and called something, and so on.

Specific-Purpose Guidelines

After you write your specific-purpose statement, use the following guidelines from Lucas (2012) as a checklist before you continue.

- **It must meet the general purpose.** The topic and specific purpose must meet the requirements of the assignment. If your general purpose is to inform, you do not want your speech to become persuasive as you prepare. The first factor to consider, so this does not occur, is to avoid certain aspect words (#3 above) such as problems, reasons, benefits, advantages, dangers, and so on. These words, when used in your specific purpose, will lead your speech down a persuasive path since they are qualifiers. In addition, some topics tend to be better suited to persuasive speeches than informative ones. For example, topics that involve some degree of controversy (you would find contradictory information when researching), seem better suited to persuasive presentations. After you have written your specific purpose, ask yourself the following question: will I want to take the extra step to ask my audience to believe or do something? If the answer is yes, go back and choose another topic for your informative speech and leave that topic for your persuasive speech.

- **It must be able to be accomplished in the time allotted.** Your purpose, or the aspect of the topic that you choose to focus on in your speech, should be sufficiently narrowed so that it can be achieved in the time you are given. Avoid the common mistake of developing specific-purpose statements that require more than the allotted speech time to achieve. Far too often, students recognize late in the preparation process that they seek to accomplish more than they have time for. After you research, you can always go back to your specific purpose and make changes to narrow it.
- **It must be relevant to my audience.** You must consider your audience when choosing the single aspect of the topic to be addressed in the speech. Specifically, what do they need or want to learn about the topic based on their knowledge and interest level? You are not building a generic speech. Instead, you are tailoring it to the specific members of your audience. You cannot just write a specific purpose without putting your audience first. As you saw in the steps of the speech-making process, you must consider your audience through the entire process. [Later chapters] will discuss how to determine what will be relevant and interesting.
- **It must not be too trivial.** Make sure that you do not choose a purpose that has little significance to your listeners. The audience has no reason to listen to a message that lacks relevance. For example, your audience does not need to learn about the parts of a backpack or how to bake a cake.
- **It must not be too technical.** Do not choose a purpose that is too specialized for your audience to readily understand. Stay away from topics and language that are "over the audience members' heads." Also, consider that the more details you include, the less time you have to explain the basics of what is necessary to understand the concepts clearly. Most often, you will not have time to deliver very technical information, regardless of how well it is explained, since you would also have to convey a great deal of basic information. You will find later in the chapter that the most important rule for an informative speech is to be clear.

Central Idea

The **central idea** of a speech is a one-sentence statement of what the speech includes, with the main points clearly stated. The main points divide the content by categorizing the information into a particular organizational pattern. The central idea is always based on the specific purpose and is shared with the audience at the end of the introduction. The goal of sharing this information with the audience is to preview the main points. Because of this, the central idea in a speech is what a thesis statement is to a paper. [Other chapters] will show you where, in your introduction, to place this central idea. Do not make writing it more difficult than it needs to be, as many students do. You will not be able to write this until you have completed your research and chosen your main points from the research. Follow the formula below to write your own central idea, and study the examples in the following section.

Aspect of Specific Purpose + Summary of Main Points

Specific Purpose: To inform my audience about the three major types of dyslexia.

Central Idea: The three major types of dyslexia are visual, auditory, and attentional.

main points

Informative Speaking

The general purpose for your first major, scholarly speech is to inform. For an informative speech, you will act as an instructor, since you will be "teaching" the audience something about the topic. After you have written a specific-purpose statement, you should then determine the type of informative speech you plan to deliver.

Types of Informative Speeches

There are four types of [informative] speeches. Your specific purpose will determine which type yours will fall under. This decision will

determine other aspects of the preparation process, such as organization. For the purposes of this course, your informative speech will be
about an object, process, event, or concept.

- **Objects**. Informative speeches about objects include anything vis-
ible and tangible. Presentations about objects can include people,
places, and things.

Specific Purpose: To inform my audience about the five major accomplishments of Jim Thorpe.

Specific Purpose: To inform my audience of the four major histori-
cal attractions in Greece.

Specific Purpose: To inform my audience about the three major
causes of endangerment of the Giant Panda in Southwest China.

- **Processes**. Informative speeches about processes include any series
of steps or stages that lead to a specific result or product. These are
usually thought of as "how-to speeches."

Specific Purpose: To inform my audience about the five major steps
of administering CPR.

Specific Purpose: To inform my audience about the four major
stages of buying a home.

Specific Purpose: To inform my audience about the three major phases of the reconstruction efforts in Haiti.

- **Events.** Informative speeches about events include occasions, incidents, or episodes. Usually an event has a beginning and an end, even if the end has not yet occurred.Specific Purpose: To inform my audience about the five major events leading up to the beginning of the Revolutionary War.

  Specific Purpose: To inform my audience about the three major holidays celebrated in Canada.

  Specific Purpose: To inform my audience about the three eras in Romanian history.

- **Concepts.** Informative speeches about concepts include any belief, theory, idea, notion, or principle. It is not something tangible that you can touch. By process of elimination, if the purpose is not an object, process, or event, it will be a concept.

  Specific Purpose: To inform my audience about the three major effects of stress.

  Specific Purpose: To inform my audience about the three major levels of Kohlberg's theory of moral development.

  Specific Purpose: To inform my audience about the five major principles ("the Five Pillars") of the Islamic faith.

Guidelines for Effective Informative Speaking

- **Be clear.** Clarifying your information clearly is your number one goal, when informing, since you cannot teach something, unless it is clear. As a teacher, your goal is not to attempt to sound smarter than your audience but to make them feel that you are one of them and are trying to make it easy for them to understand. Use the following ways to accomplish this:
  - **Explain thoroughly.** You do not want the audience to be more confused at the end of your speech than they were before your speech. Think about your objective as putting a puzzle together

to give your audience a full picture. Use a balance of basics and specifics. If your purpose is to discuss how to solve the crisis in Liberia, you will have to give enough background information, in the beginning and as you go, about what is happening there.

- **Avoid being technical.** Many students like to use very technical terms when writing papers and feel that they must do the same in a speech. However, if clarity is the goal, then you want to use the simplest terms possible so the audience will not be confused. If you already know a great deal about your topic, you may find it difficult to "dumb down" more technical information into terms they identify with. Avoid using technical terms that your audience will not understand. As you are searching for information, consider paraphrasing complicated material in order for your audience to comprehend the content more quickly and more easily. Remember that they are hearing much of this information for the first time and they only hear it once.

- **Compare and contrast.** You want to avoid being vague. The best way to prevent abstractness is to use description by comparing and contrasting your ideas. Compare or contrast the concept with something the audience is already familiar with. Creating examples will help to do this. You could say, "It is like this" or "It is different in this way."

- **Be relevant.** Your speech must not be generic in nature. You will tailor the content of the speech to your specific audience. If that audience were to change, you would need to adapt your message to new demographic and situational factors. You will be expected to explain to the audience why the material you are presenting should mean something to them and why they should learn the information. Make clear to the audience how the topic affects them and how they can use it. Adapting your message to the audience will be discussed in greater detail in [later chapters].

- **Do not overestimate what the audience knows.** It is easy to assume that because you know a lot about the topic, your audience does, too. However, in many cases this is a faulty assumption. You will become an "expert" with the content of your speech, but you must take a step back in order to begin to understand how to share basic information with your audience. [Other chapters] will teach you how to gather information about your audience so you can determine their knowledge level.

- **Report accurately.** As an informative speaker, you are passing information from sources to your audience. When doing this, make sure that you are conveying the supporting materials truthfully and accurately to your listeners. You will be expected to check all information before you report it in your speech. [Other chapters] will discuss how to do this.

- **Personalize your ideas.** Present your thoughts in human terms that relate to the experiences of the audience. Do not be afraid to use your own experiences to bring life to your information. You want the audience to identify with you and your speech, so learn what experiences are common to you and the audience members. We will discuss how to do this in more detail in the following chapters.

Persuasive Speaking

By Amy Muckleroy Carwile

In this chapter are three sections. The first section will give you a short history of persuasion, some of the individuals that first studied persuasion, and the effects of persuasive messages. You will find working definitions of persuasion, coercion, and propaganda. You will also find information about how attitudes, values, and beliefs relate to persuasive speaking. Beginning in the second section, you will find information about constructing an argument and avoiding fallacies. You will also learn about Maslow's Hierarchy of Needs (Maslow, 1970), Social Judgment Theory (Sherif & Hovland, 1961), and the Elaboration Likelihood Model (Petty & Cacioppo, 1986). The final section gives specific directions for structuring persuasive speeches according to the Problem–Cause–Solution pattern and using Monroe's Motivated Sequence (Monroe, 1935). After completion of this lesson, you should have the necessary tools to construct a logically sound, emotionally compelling, and credible persuasive speech.

History of Persuasion

As you begin to learn about something that may be new to you, it helps to understand the background or history of a topic. Persuasion and persuasive speaking is not a new concept or idea. It has been around for many centuries. Greek teachers called *Sophists* were paid teachers of rhetoric. Sophists did not believe, as some Greek citizens did, that persuasion is an art. Thus, the Sophists taught leading Greek citizens the skills needed by an orator for success in the political climate of the day (Perloff, 2008).

At approximately this same time, Plato, a Greek philosopher, es-poused his beliefs that persuasion (as taught by the Sophists) was an effort to hide the truth from the audience. Plato believed that truth was an important value. He further advocated that speakers should seek the truth and deliver this truth to an audience. Only then could a speaker be a competent and worthy orator (Perloff, 2008). As a student in a public speaking course, you are probably wondering why you should even care about this. It is because this debate continues even [today]. It is also because persuasive speaking can be difficult to learn and individuals have seen persuasive speaking used in a negative way. Thus, some individuals may perceive persuasion as a skill anyone can learn that they could used for nefarious purposes, and other individuals perceive persuasion as an art to be appreciated and lauded. When you think about persuasive speaking, which position do you think is correct? Are there extenuating circumstances, which make persuasion a skill or an art? By the time that you finish this chapter, you will see that persuasion has elements of both.

Aristotle and Logos, Pathos, Ethos

In the section about the public speaking intersection, you read about Aristotle's views regarding logos, pathos, and ethos. Remember that the definition of logos was a speech that was well structured and argued logically. Pathos, according to Aristotle, meant that a speaker should appeal to the audience's emotions, and ethos was a speaker's credibility as perceived by the audience. *The Works of Aristotle, Volume II* (1971) defined rhetoric as "the faculty of discovering in any particular case all of the available means of persuasion" and offered that for a speech to be effective, it should contain each of these types of appeals. As he studied oratory, Aristotle recognized that adapting a message to a particular audience's needs was also a necessary part of persuasive speaking. By understanding a bit about the history of persuasion and some of the philosophers who studied it, you should be able to create a persuasive message more effectively.

Persuasion—Defined

Many communication scholars have sought to define and draw up a plan for executing a persuasive message. Hamilton (2009) offers that "persuasion is communication that is intended to influence choice" (p. 283). Persuasion is "the process of influencing other people's attitudes, beliefs, values, or behaviors" (Sellnow, 2005, p. G5). Simonds, Hunt, and Simonds (2010) suggest that a persuasive speech is one "that is controversial in some way and attempts to influence the audience's attitudes, beliefs, or actions with regard to the issue; typically about current events, social issues, local issues, or beliefs" (p. 282). All of these are important contributions to the study of persuasion and persuasive speaking. However, for this [chapter], the definition we will use is Perloff's. He defines *persuasion* "as a symbolic process in which communicators try to convince other people to change their attitudes or behaviors regarding an issue through the transmission of a message in an atmosphere of free choice" (p. 17).

To truly understand Perloff's definition of persuasion, it should be dismantled a piece at a time. First, persuasion is "a symbolic process." This means that a speaker uses words to create a message processed by an audience. The words selected, the structure of the speech, even the delivery of the speech, are all part of this symbolic process. From an audience's standpoint, how the words are interpreted, whether the structure and delivery are deemed appropriate and effective, is part of the process. Remember that you learned about the functions of language as arbitrary and symbolic. Recall too, that communication is not stagnant; it is a continually evolving process intent on shared meaning.

The next component of Perloff's definition is that "communicators try to convince other people." Just as the Sophists taught a skill to ancient Greeks for influencing the electorate, a persuasive speaker has a specific goal in mind. For example, a car salesperson has the goal of influencing your behavior to buy a certain model of automobile and attempts to accomplish the goal by creating a persuasive message.

Another example could be something like this: you call your parents because your bank balance is low. This has been a particularly expensive week because attending the football game on Saturday demanded a new outfit, and all of your textbooks finally came in and had to be paid for. Therefore, you create a persuasive message with the intention of getting an influx of cash deposited into your bank account. Persuasion is INTENTIONAL, and your audience knows this. It is accepted by the audience that you are presenting an argument to convince them. Plato would be happy with your efforts because you are not hiding the truth or attempting to persuade in an unethical way; you are up front and honest about your intentions.

Not only is a persuasive speech created with intent, the goal is to get your audience to "change their attitudes or behaviors regarding an issue" (Perloff, 2008). You want your audience to do something (or not do something), and there is an explicit call to action in a persuasive speech. Suppose your persuasive speech is about alternatives to bottled water. You could say, "Americans buy an estimated 29.8 billion plastic water bottles every year and nearly eight out of every 10 bottles will end up in a landfill" (United States Environmental Protection Agency). The ultimate goal of your persuasive speech is to urge the audience to buy and use a reusable water bottle. Your goal is to cause an audience member to change their behavior.

Perloff suggests that individuals actually persuade themselves, and that happens when persuasive speakers provide the arguments effectively (p. 19). His idea supports the Sophist's view that if a persuasive speaker employs all the necessary tools, he is able to create a persuasive message that gets the audience to act in the way he advocates in his speech.

Obviously, persuasion cannot occur without a message, and Perloff's definition included the following: "through the transmission of a message." As a persuasive speaker, you transmit your message verbally and nonverbally. Refer to [later chapters] to study more about your delivery and make the appropriate adjustments in your verbal and nonverbal delivery to enhance your persuasive message. Transmission of a persuasive message can occur via mass communication channels or interpersonally. Your message may be logically organized and structured (logos) and emotionally relevant to your audience (pathos), but you may lack the credibility (ethos) to deliver the message. Does that mean that you did not transmit a message? No. Think about the last advertisement you saw that caused you to reject the product just because you did not like the celebrity endorsing the product. If you rejected buying Nike products because you did not like Tiger Woods, does that mean that Nike did not transmit a message?

Absolutely not. The message was transmitted, but you rejected the message because it lacked one of Aristotle's essential parts, ethos.

The last part of Perloff's definition of persuasion includes the phrase "in an atmosphere of free choice." This is not unlike the idea that an audience persuades themselves, because with a persuasive message, your audience makes a conscious decision to agree or disagree with your message. In the case of the car salesperson, if you feel pressured to purchase, you may not buy the new car. On the other hand, if the salesperson offers information, appeals to your emotions, reminds you of someone you trust by cultivating a positive ethos, and gives you time to think over your purchase, you may be more likely to buy the car.

Persuasion, Coercion, and Propaganda

So what happens if persuasion crosses the line and becomes what Plato feared—dishonest and ethically at odds with the truth? Is that persuasion or coercion? Where is the line between persuasion and coercion? At what point does persuasion become propaganda? First, you must realize that there really is no proverbial line in the sand between persuasion and coercion. Ultimately, the audience makes a decision about whether they were persuaded or coerced. *Coercion* means to use force or intimidation to gain compliance. This means that coercion forces audience members to change a behavior or an attitude, usually under duress. Coercion then, is contrary to persuasion because persuasion allows an audience member to freely choose to accept or reject your position or call to action.

Propaganda is another term that unfortunately is often used synonymously with persuasion. Propaganda, according to Perloff, has four elements that make it very different from persuasion. First, propaganda is "typically invoked to describe mass influence through mass media" (Perloff, 2008). Persuasion can happen via mass media channels, but also happens interpersonally. Propaganda rarely happens interpersonally. Plato would not be a fan of propaganda because it is "covert" (Perloff, 2008, p. 33). If you are involved in propaganda, the truth and intention of your message is hidden from your audience. Remember that persuasion is intentional and your audience is aware that you are trying to persuade them about your topic, which is contrary to propaganda.

If your message is propaganda, you are the sole controller of information. This is the third difference between persuasion and propaganda. Essentially, this means that you have eliminated your audience's option to freely choose the messages they consume or accept. Consider this: the current administration of your country owns and controls the

ONE television channel where you can get information. You do not have access to the Internet except through filters controlled by your government. The only information you can find here is always positive regarding the administration. *Propaganda* means that a single source controls all the information available to the public, and usually that information is positively slanted toward the source of the information.

Lastly, the connotation of the word propaganda is negative, while the connotation of the word persuasion is typically positive (Perloff, 2008, p. 33). *Connotation* means that words have a meaning besides the explicit meaning of the word. In other words, connotation is the emotional connection we have to a word. *Denotation* is the dictionary definition of a word. For example, consider the word *home*. From a definition or denotative standpoint, *home* can be the city and state you live in or grew up in, or your living space. From a connotative standpoint, *home* may be the place that you feel completely safe and secure, like Dorothy in the Wizard of Oz.

Attitudes, Beliefs, and Values

Throughout this chapter, you have learned about logos, pathos, and ethos as well as persuasion, coercion, and propaganda. Most of the information in this section of the chapter described how persuasion attempts to influence the attitudes, beliefs, or values of your audience.

Recall that an *attitude* is an inclination to respond positively or negatively to a speaker or a topic. Attitudes of your audience can be easily discovered using questionnaires and surveys, or by simply asking the right question, and can be changed with a solid message well delivered by a competent speaker with a positive ethos.

Beliefs are not as easy to change as attitudes because *beliefs* are principles a listener always regards as true. Changing someone's beliefs takes much more work on a speaker's part.

Values are beliefs that regulate our attitudes and are deeply ingrained, culturally bound, and not likely to change. Our attitudes and beliefs connect to our values. Our values are the things that we learn through our interaction with our families, our schools, and our religion. These values help us formulate our beliefs and our attitudes.

Now that you have the background and definition of persuasion, the next step in becoming an effective persuasive speaker is to cover important information regarding some theories of persuasion. The next section of this chapter details how to construct arguments while avoiding fallacies.

Arguments

Remember that the elements of our definition of persuasion require intent to change an attitude or a behavior through a message, with the understanding that the audience is completely knowledgeable of the speaker's intent. Persuading your audience begins with your argument. An *argument* is "a set of claims, one of which is meant to be supported by the others" (Munson & Black, 2007).

Think of your persuasive speech as an argument pyramid. The top of the pyramid is the goal of your persuasive speech and the supporting claims form the base levels of your pyramid. You cannot build a stable pyramid without a solid base structure. Suppose you have chosen to persuade your audience that volunteering in your community has many benefits, including network contacts, better overall health, and giving the volunteer the opportunity to learn new skills. Your argument pyramid would look something like the figure below. Look closely at the diagram. Each main point is dependent on the other. If one main point fails, you cannot reach your goal.

Each of the supporting claims becomes a main point for your persuasive speech. You will need research to help you support each of the main points in your speech.

Arguments involve another important element: your audience and their reasoning. As you speak, your audience is involved in reasoning. Reasoning is a process of developing judgments or inferences using facts. This means that your audience is mentally evaluating your argument pyramid as you speak and deciding if you supported your goal adequately based on your argument. This cognitive process is inference. If you are successful, your audience evaluates you (ethos), your argument or logic (logos), and your emotional appeal (pathos) as sufficient to support the argument of your speech: to persuade them to volunteer.

Fallacies

In the perfect persuasive world, everything works just like described above. However, reasoning does not always happen easily and inferences may get sidetracked. Fallacies are what cause inferences to be sidetracked. By definition, a *fallacy* is an error in reasoning that makes arguments illogical and unsound. Post hoc, begging the question, ad hominem, ad verecundiam, and slippery slope are all fallacies that can inhibit your goal of persuasive speaking.

Post Hoc

A *post hoc* fallacy means that one event preceded a second event. Because the second event followed the first event, individuals assume that the first event caused the second. This may sound confusing, so think about it this way. Suppose you are a golfer who owns a lucky pair of shoes and when you wear the lucky shoes, you always win the golf match. This is a post hoc fallacy. The first event is that you wear the shoes. The second event is that you win. The inference you make is that the shoes actually helped you win the match. Logically, wearing a certain pair of shoes did not cause you to win. What really happened was that you played better than your opponent, and that was why you won. In a persuasive speech, the lucky shoes logic will not work. You must rely on solid arguments.

Begging the Question

Another fallacy persuasive speakers should avoid is begging the question. *Begging the question* means that the speaker assumes something is a fact when the fact has not been proven to be a fact. There is a large difference between a fact and an opinion. A *fact* is something that can be proven true or false and verified with evidence. An *opinion* is an expression of feelings that cannot be proven true or false. In persuasive speaking, the speaker is likely to use emotional appeals, and audience members should be careful to discern which information is and is not fact-based. A persuasive speaker could do this by making a stereotypical remark without conducting appropriate analysis. For example, a speaker could say, "We are all against gay marriage here in our state." The speaker's audience may have many audience members who support gay marriage, but because the speaker did not conduct the appropriate audience analysis, he used fallacious reasoning called begging the question. In other words, he made an inaccurate comment based on his feelings (opinion), not a proven fact. Thus, he lost the opportunity to persuade his audience.

Ad Hominem

An *ad hominem* fallacy means that the speaker demeans the person making an argument rather than attacking the argument made by the person. Think of ad hominem in a political debate. Mr. Brown demeans Mr. Black, personally, rather than attacking Mr. Black's argument or political record. Imagine this scenario: Mr. Black touts his experience as head of the city's transportation department. During his tenure there, he balanced the transportation departmental budget by upgrading the light rail system and adding train stops. The light rail system helped commuters in the city because Mr. Black reduced the train fare and more people rode the train. The increase in revenue from ticketed passengers and commuter passes helped balance the transportation department's budget. Mr. Brown ignores the positive points related to Mr. Black's record of a balanced budget and attacks Mr. Black on a personal level by alleging an affair with an intern in the transportation department. In an election year in the United States, ad hominem fallacies abound in candidates' ads. The next time you watch a debate see if anyone engages in the ad hominem fallacy.

Ad Verecundiam

Another fallacy that you should be aware of is *ad verecundiam*. This fallacy means a speaker appeals to an authority figure as argument support based solely on the individual's position as an authority figure, not because the authority is an expert in relation to your topic. For example, you decide that you can persuade your audience to drink less coffee because the Dean of your college advocates the behavior. Unless your Dean is a recently retired physician, she is probably not an expert on the potential health benefits of drinking more water daily. Your argument support would be stronger if you found a more logical person to endorse your position on the dangers of caffeine abuse.

Slippery Slope

The *slippery slope* fallacy may be easiest to define because it means that a speaker suggests one particular action will set a series of actions in motion, which results in an inevitable and often unpleasant conclusion. Again, political opponents use the slippery slope  fallacy. As an example, Candidate Smith's platform calls for the registration of all handguns. Candidate Jones uses the slippery slope fallacy to suggest that if everyone is required to register all their handguns, it could lead to: 1) only criminals having access to guns,

2) the required registration of hunting rifles 3) citizens losing the constitutional right to bear arms, and 4) all citizens becoming defenseless in their own homes. As a beginning speaker, if you are not careful, you may mistakenly use the slippery slope fallacy in a persuasive speech. Make sure you verify your facts and do not engage in fallacious reasoning.

All of these fallacies can ruin your persuasive argument and cause you to miss your goal. However, you now have the knowledge to avoid fallacious reasoning. The next section of this chapter explains a few theories of persuasion and offers some ideas about structuring a persuasive speech based on these theoretical perspectives.

Persuasive Theoretical Perspectives

Maslow and NEEDS

Persuasive speakers can appeal to an audience's needs as a persuasive strategy. Abraham Maslow (1970) suggested that this is an ideal way to persuade individuals. Over thirty years ago, he devised a hierarchy of needs based on his psychological research. Even [today], persuaders can still use these ideas effectively in persuasive speaking by appealing to listeners' needs. Maslow's concept centers around the idea that a listener's needs begin with the physiological. Next a person seeks satisfaction of safety, social, and self esteem needs. Finally, once these four needs are met, a person attempts to satisfy the self-actualization need. A persuasive speaker can focus his speech on these needs as a way to persuade effectively. Figure 10-1 represents the *Hierarchy of Needs* developed by Maslow. His design suggests that the most necessary and important needs are at the bottom of the figure and that successive needs can be met as each lower level need becomes satisfied.

Physiological needs are our most basic. Things like fresh air, food, water, and shelter are all physiological needs. Potentially, you could structure a persuasive speech using these needs as a focus if your audience has not had food or water in a week. Your audience might be willing to do whatever you suggest to obtain food or water. However, should you choose to structure a speech in this way, you have crossed the line between persuasion and coercion. This would be unethical. Is there a way to structure a speech appealing to the audience's physiological needs and not compromise your ethics? One way would be to appeal to your audience to eat healthier. This would not compromise your ethics as a speaker.

Figure 10-1   Maslow's Hierarchy of Needs

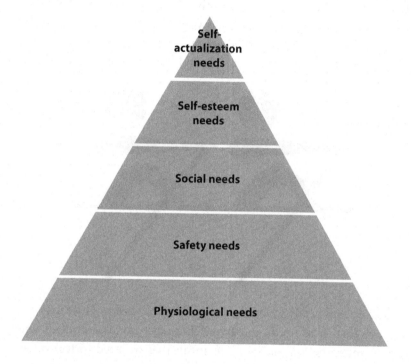

The second level needs, according to Maslow, are safety or security needs. *Safety* or security needs are confidence in our safety and security. This means things like the safety of our neighborhood and the security of our job, which allows us to meet our financial obligations. We may feel the need to move to another neighborhood or even another city if the crime rates are increasing and we believe our job is secure enough to support a move. Creating a persuasive speech around these needs could focus on reducing crime in your neighborhood or near your university.

Our social needs come at the third level of Maslow's hierarchy. Human beings have a desire to feel like we belong. That is, our *social needs* are that we want to feel as if we have connections with others. As an example, you need to present a persuasive speech for a group of parents at a university recruiting event. You could focus on meeting this need for potential students. In general, parents want to know that their child will be able to connect with a group of students with similar interests. Explaining the many ways your university helps new freshmen get involved could persuade parents that their child will have a place there because his or her social needs will be met.

Self-esteem needs are on the fourth level of Maslow's hierarchy. He suggests that these needs go beyond finding a group of students with similar interests. *Self-esteem needs* mean that we need to feel valued by others. For example, you have a particularly demanding job and all the members of your work team overlook your contributions to the company. You could be susceptible to a persuasive speech by another company offering you a new position. This new company could be effective by appealing to your self-esteem needs in this situation because they are unfulfilled.

The highest level of need is what Maslow calls *self-actualization*. This type of need means that we achieve a dream or we accomplish a goal we set for ourselves. In order to create a persuasive speech targeted toward your audience's self-actualization needs, all audience members need to hold analogous goals or dreams. Consider this example: you work for a company specializing in teaching people to fly an airplane. All people in your audience are interested in this as well. Because they are already interested, it may be easier to persuade them to invest their time and money if you focus your speech on the self-actualization needs. These needs can be the benefits a person can obtain by having a private pilot's license. If you presented this speech to your public speaking class, you would have more difficulty, because they would be a captive audience.

Use Maslow's hierarchy to help you focus your persuasive speech on the audience's needs. Conducting a complete audience analysis will provide you with information about their needs and the ways you can fulfill them using Maslow's ideas.

Social Judgment Theory and Latitudes

Another concept regarding persuasion focuses on Sherif and Hovland's Social Judgment Theory (1961). *Social Judgment Theory* offers that as someone encounters a persuasive message, he or she categorizes it as acceptable or something we will reject because of our attitudes related to the topic. Additionally, Social Judgment Theory suggests persuasion can occur only if the attitude presented for consideration is close to what the listener currently believes. Latitudes of acceptance, rejection, and non-commitment are central components of Social Judgment Theory.

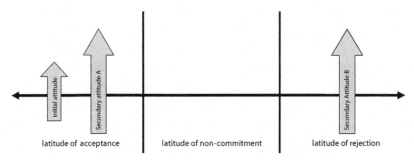

latitude of acceptance   latitude of non-commitment   latitude of rejection

All latitudes fall on a continuum. The *latitude of acceptance* is a range of all acceptable attitudes regarding a particular topic. The *latitude of rejection* is a range of all non-acceptable attitudes regarding a particular topic. The *latitude of non-commitment* is a range on the continuum indicating that your audience feels neither positively nor negatively about your topic.

Notice that in the figure representing the concepts of Social Judgment Theory, the three latitudes are portrayed as a continuum with sections marked for each latitude. While the drawing represents rigid boundaries for latitudes, latitudes in this case have permeable boundaries that are constantly changing and overlapping each other. The drawing is a visual representation of the conceptual ideas of the theory.

The three arrows show initial attitude, secondary attitude A, and secondary attitude B. The initial attitude represents the attitude of your audience about your topic, which you obtained through audience analysis. If the target of your persuasive speech aims toward Secondary Attitude A, you are more likely to accomplish your persuasive goal rather than if you target a persuasive message at Secondary Attitude B. There are two reasons for this.

First, if your persuasive message targets the attitude close to your audience's initial attitude, you should have much less difficulty advocating for a particular choice. A second reason is that Secondary Attitude A is within your audience's latitude of acceptance. If your persuasive message focuses on Secondary Attitude B, you have entered the audience's latitude of rejection. This creates a large distance between the audience's initial attitude and the attitude you advocate. These two issues can make persuasion very difficult. Think about your persuasive message. Could you utilize the information you just learned about Social Judgment theory to help you organize your message? Examine the following scenario for a more complete understanding regarding the theory's concepts.

You are trying to persuade your audience that President Barack Obama's handling of British Petroleum's 2010 oil spill in the Gulf of Mexico was appropriate. Some individuals in your audience believe that Mr. Obama did all that he could do to help get Americans the help they needed. Their initial attitude is within the latitude of acceptance. Other individuals in your audience believe that Mr. Obama mishandled the problem because he offered no real solutions to prevent future oil spills in the Gulf. Some of your audience members holding this attitude have beach houses as investments, and their revenue streams diminished during the summer of 2010 because of the spill. This means that their initial position is solidly entrenched in the latitude of rejection. Other audience members may not have an opinion about the issue. Their initial attitude position is within the latitude of non-commitment.

If you conducted audience analysis, you will have the benefit of this information about your audience members' attitudes related to your topic. As you begin to construct your persuasive speech, consider the concepts of Social Judgment Theory and structure your persuasive speech for maximum impact. You should target your speech toward those individuals whose initial attitude position is near your own and within the latitude of acceptance to have the greatest change of success.

Elaboration Likelihood Model and Processing

The last theory of persuasion presented in this [chapter] deals with how audiences process persuasive messages, not latitudes or needs. The *Elaboration Likelihood Model* (ELM) examines how individuals cognitively process a persuasive message (Petty & Cacioppo, 1986).

In this model, *elaboration* refers to the amount of cognitive resources a person devotes to message processing. Petty and Cacioppo suggest audience members process (or elaborate) persuasive messages in one of two ways: peripherally or low, and centrally or high.

Peripheral or low-message processing occurs when the audience elaborates in a superficial manner in relation to a persuasive message. Peripheral processing means that the audience member makes a snap judgment and does not carefully evaluate or critically analyze your argument, or any emotional appeals. However, if the audience perceives you as a credible speaker, this can work in your favor because they are using peripheral processing. Your attractiveness, delivery (verbal and nonverbal), clothing choices, and demeanor are the elements your audience uses most often to process a message when they engage in peripheral (or low) elaboration. If your audience member were peripherally processing your message, you would be wise to be dressed appropriately for your presentation. In addition, an animated, dynamic delivery will also increase the chances of success in this case.

One the other hand, *central* or high-message processing occurs when the audience elaborates thoroughly and critically in relation to a persuasive message. Critically analyzing your message means that your audience carefully evaluates your argument and the supporting documentation you have presented. They also determine if your message is a well-organized persuasive presentation. Audiences involved in critically analyzing your message, or central elaboration, will undoubtedly interpret your argument and examine your message for logos, pathos, and ethos. When your topic is controversial, you should deliberately plan, scrupulously research, and precisely organize your persuasive message. Your delivery is important, but when your audience is involved in central processing, they are more actively involved in critical thinking. In this instance, you cannot rely solely on your dynamism or ethos as a speaker. You must make your appeal to the audience based on their cognitive processing of your message.

As you choose your persuasive topic and structure your speech, think carefully about how the Elaboration Likelihood Model can help guide your choices and the construction of your persuasive speech.

Consider the following scenario. You have chosen the economic situation in the United States as a persuasive speech topic. Because this topic is timely, you can assume your audience will elaborate about this controversial topic using central message processing. In order to persuade your audience effectively, your argument must be sound, well researched, and supported with sources your audience will perceive as credible. You will also need to be dynamic and credible as you deliver your speech, but because the audience will be using central processing, this may be less important.

Another example surrounds a less controversial persuasive topic such as persuading your classmates to sign a petition to pressure the administration to add another student parking lot at your university. In this case, your dynamic presentation and positive ethos will be much more important, as your audience engages in peripheral or low elaboration about your message. Your speech still needs to be structured and organized well, but charisma and credibility of the speaker are paramount, as the audience uses peripheral elaboration. Usually a message aimed at peripheral processing is not a critically important topic. In other words, it would be unethical for you to target a message for peripheral processing if you were discussing the importance of signing a living will because this is a serious topic. Ethically, you could aim for signing a petition similar to the scenario above if you choose to target the audience's peripheral cognitive elaboration.

This section has covered several important ideas about persuasive theories, arguments, and fallacies, and you have a good idea about how to create an exceptional persuasive speech. Next, you will gather information about some more tools to help you begin to structure a persuasive message. You will find step-by-step organizing tools in the next section.

Organizational Structures

There are many ways to organize persuasive speeches. However, [in this chapter], only two structures are presented. If you conduct research and find another structure you think lends itself to your particular topic, discuss it with your professor. The two structures included here are: 1) The Problem–Cause–Solution structure and 2) the Motivated Sequence. Both are common organizational patterns used by beginning public speakers to help structure persuasive speeches.

Problem–Cause–Solution Structure

Problem–Cause–Solution is an ideal organizational structure used for highlighting a specific problem or issue facing society. If you use this structure for your speech, you will clearly outline the Problem, the Cause, and the Solution. This structure can help the audience contemplate and think critically about your topic. This structure helps easily organize the main points in the body of your speech. Main point 1 is the problem, main point 2 is the cause, and main point 3 is the solution. Below are a general explanation and a detailed example of this organizational structure to help you understand it more fully.

BASIC STRUCTURE FOR A PROBLEM-CAUSE-SOLUTION SPEECH

Introduction

Body

MP1: **PROBLEM** - State your problem clearly and make sure you talk about why your topic is a problem and how it is a problem for your audience.

[Transition]

MP2: **CAUSE** - Explain the cause (or causes) of your problem and give reasons and/or examples demonstrating the cause of the problem. Be sure to relate these causes to your audience.

[Transition]

MP3: **SOLUTION** - Offer your solution to the problem in this main point. In a persuasive speech, be sure to discuss any solutions that have been proposed, even if you disagree with the. This will give you the opportunity to explain why your solution is the best option for solving the problem for your audience.

Conclusion

Use the example below to see a more complete body of a persuasive speech about childhood obesity using the problem-cause-solution organizational structure.

PROBLEM–CAUSE–SOLUTION SPEECH

TOPIC: Childhood Obesity
INTRODUCTION
BODY

I.   PROBLEM:
       Childhood obesity is a problem at a critical point in the United States. Children in the US need our help. Our current health care system is overwhelmed, stemming from obesity. Diabetes, high cholesterol, and high blood pressure can be traced to obesity in adults, and now even in children these diseases are becoming worrisome. Sometimes childhood can be difficult, but suffering through it because of a preventable problem—obesity—seems to put many children at risk of ridicule by their peers, which could lead to other difficulties for them.

TRANSITION

II.   CAUSE:
       There are some causes of childhood obesity that are easy to pinpoint. Sometimes childhood obesity is caused by too little regular exercise. Add this to poor nutrition as another cause. Other causes of childhood obesity can be genetic diseases or hormone abnormalities.

TRANSITION

III.   SOLUTION:
       If your child has a genetic disease or a hormone abnormality, seek appropriate medical care and medication. This could be the answer for your child. For other children,

focus on teaching them to eat healthier meals and encourage regular exercising. These two solutions are both viable and can help combat this debilitating epidemic.

CONCLUSION

The Motivated Sequence Structure

Another common form for structuring persuasive speeches is *Monroe's Motivated Sequence*. Dr. Alan Monroe developed a design plan for arranging persuasive speeches and published his method in *The Principles and Types of Speeches* in 1935. Even though this book is decades old, the concept is alive, well, and in use today.

You probably have never noticed the Motivated Sequence, but most likely you see it daily as you watch television. The Motivated Sequence is used commonly in advertisements. Think about the last advertisement you saw on television or heard on the radio as you read about the five steps in the Motivated Sequence: Attention, Need, Satisfaction, Visualization, and Action.

The attention step in the Motivated Sequence gives a hint to the purpose of your speech. The *attention step* is your attention getting device. This step belongs in the introduction portion of your speech. If you do not get the audience's attention and maintain it, they could miss your entire speech. This puts you at risk of not meeting your persuasive goal.

The *need step* in the Motivated Sequence emphasizes a single issue that the audience needs to attend to. This step is not unlike the problem step in the problem–cause–solution organizational structure. You present the audience with a need only they can fulfill. You must generate this unfulfilled need in your audience by using appropriate style and delivery. This step also belongs in the introduction portion of your speech.

The Motivated Sequence's third step is satisfaction. This step begins the body section of your speech. Remember that you have created an unfulfilled need that only the audience can satisfy. The *satisfaction step* is the place you help the audience satisfy or fulfill the need you created in the previous step. Your speech will advocate for a change in belief, attitude, or behavior based on the way your idea can satisfy the need you have created in your audience.

Visualization is the next step in the Motivated Sequence and is included as part of the body of the speech. This section also employs descriptive language and style for maximum effectiveness. The *visualization step* is the place you create a mental image of the proposed solution, or your audience should visualize how they can personally benefit from satisfying the need you created. Remember [to address] the audience's mentality of [W.I.I.F.M.] (what's in it for me?). Your ethical responsibility to your audience should meet this expectation. You can also describe how the audience may encounter difficulties if they choose not to adopt your solution. Be creative and use particularly vivid language in this step to help create the visual image.

The final step in the Motivated Sequence is the action step. The *action step* is your call to action and is part of the conclusion portion of your speech. This step is the place in the speech that asks the audience to do something or believe something based on the sound argument, the structure, and the supporting documentation you presented to them. Once you make the call to action, remember to conclude your speech by returning to the attention-getting device you used in the introduction. Doing this reinforces the main points and brings your argument full circle. See Figure 10-2 to see how the steps in the Motivated Sequence fit into the three main components of a speech.

Figure 10-2 Components of a Speech and the Motivated Sequence

As you have learned throughout this chapter, persuasion is not easy to define and can be difficult for a novice speaker to accomplish. This chapter provided information about the history, background, and definition of persuasion. Persuasive theories, fallacies, beliefs, values, and attitudes are all important concepts for you to remember as you construct a persuasive speech. You now have the tools to construct a persuasive speech based on your audience's needs, latitudes, or message processing. In addition, this chapter outlined two different organizational structures for persuasive speeches. You are now ready to move on to the next chapter.

Glossary

Action step
Ad hominem
Ad [vericundiam]
[Argument]
Attention step
Attitudes
Begging the question
Belief
Central processing
Coercion
[Connotation]

[Denotation]
Elaboration
ELM
[Fact]
Fallacy
Hierarchy of needs
Latitude of acceptance
Latitude of non-commitment
Latitude of rejection
Motivated sequence
Need step
Opinion
Peripheral processing
Persuasion
Physiological needs
Post hoc
Propaganda
Safety needs
Satisfaction step
Self-actualization needs
Self-esteem needs
Slippery slope
Social judgment theory
Social needs
Sophists
Value
Visualization step

References

Hamilton, C. (2009). *Essentials of public speaking* (4th ed.). Boston, MA: Wadsworth.

Monroe, A. (1935). *The principles and types of speeches*. Chicago, IL: Scott, Foresman.

Perloff, R. (2008). *The dynamics of persuasion: Communication and attitudes in the 21st century* (3rd ed.). New York, NY: Routledge.

Petty, R., & Cacioppo, J. (1986). *Communications and persuasion*. New York, NY: Springer-Verlag.

Sellnow, D. (2005). *Confident public speaking* (2nd ed.). Belmont, CA: Thomson.

Sherif, M., & Hovland, C. (1961). *Social judgement: Assimilation and contrast effects in communication and attitude change*. New Haven, CT: Yale University Press.

Simonds, C., Hunt, S., & Simonds, B. (2010). *Public speaking: Prepare, present, participate*. Boston, MA: Allyn & Bacon.

Photo Credits

Pictograms of Olympic Sports - Rowing: http://commons.wikimedia.org/wiki/File:Rowing_pictogram.svg. Copyright in the Public Domain.

Cessna 172 (C-GDQG): http://commons.wikimedia.org/wiki/File:GDQG.jpg. Copyright in the Public Domain.

Brad Pitt, Matt Damon, and George Clooney Tour Incirlik Air Base, Turkey, on December 7 to Show Appreciation for U.S. Troops: http://commons.wikimedia.org/wiki/File:Pitt_Clooney_Damon.jpg. Copyright in the Public Domain.

Governor Rick Perry Speaking at the Houston Technology Center: Copyright © (CC by 2.0) at Source: http://www.flickr.com/photos/16638697@N00/5047775028.

Part III

Delivering Powerful Presentations

Mastering Vocal Eloquence: Public Performance and Oral Interpretation

By John Ross, Jr.

"Eloquence, indeed, does not consist in speech. It cannot be brought from far. Labor and learning may toil for it, but they will toil in vain. Words and phrases may be marshaled in every way, but they cannot compass it. It must exist in the man, in the subject, and in the occasion."

—Daniel Webster, 19th century American statesmen and orator

A Short Bit of Vocal Eloquence (Expressive) Theory

In many ways, your actual voice itself is more important than any script you may perform onstage in a play, the text of a speech you may give before an audience, or the actual words you may use during a formal or informal interview or casual conversation. The human voice is quite dynamic. This means that, by your voice alone, you can be piercing, strident, soft, yielding, sighing, or screeching. The human voice can growl, suggest, recommend, claim, or demand. As a speaker you have the potential to assert, proclaim, allege, declare, and even affirm. When your voice implies meaning, we call it paralanguage. *Paralanguage* is the audible constituents that accompany speech, which in turn *decrease* or *increase* the meanings of words and sentences. Paralanguage includes your *pitch,* your *volume,* and, in most cases, the *inflection* and *intentionality* of speech. Paralanguage is not about what you say but *how* you say it.

From the resonance of your voice alone, your listeners will make conclusions about your way of thinking about them, and the thoughts you are hoping to present. *Resonance* is the magnification and adjustment of the sound of your voice by an air-filled chamber or *cavity* of your body, such as your chest, throat, mouth, or nasal cavity.

Furthermore, by the very resonance of your voice alone, your listeners will be able to judge your *authenticity, sincerity,* and *credibility.* In short, your voice will directly *or* indirectly shape how your listeners will act in response to you and your words, irrespective of what you say.

Understanding the correct use of your voice can highlight, and in turn strengthen, every script, speech, or daily conversation in which you partake.

If the pitch, volume, rhythm, and timbre of your voice never fluctuate, you'll be speaking in what we term as *monotone.* As a result, you risk losing the attention of your listeners from the get-go.

When you are monotonous, it puts forward to your listeners that you have little invested in them or in your message. It says to them that perhaps you really do not care very much about what they may think or feel or how they may choose to respond.

An expressive or *eloquent voice* pauses and speeds up, changes pace, lowers and raises volume, and varies in pitch. It is interested in conveying emotion and passion.

On no account should you ever be monotone onstage, while giving a speech, during an interview, or, for that matter, even in your daily conversations. Your voice (not *what* you say) is the instrument with which you ultimately communicate. Practice controlling and managing your unique instrument.

Exercise 1: Being Heard by All Is Always the First Rule

This simple classroom or at-home exercise can be used to help stimulate you with energy whenever needed. It is ideal before classroom participation. It helps you prepare properly in class to make noisy sounds, vowels, consonants and to speak more clearly by increasing your *volume*.

Remember that no matter where you are or what you may be speaking about, if you cannot be heard by all, you are wasting both your own time and that of your listeners.

Improving your volume allows the articulation of individual words to be heard more easily. Raising the volume of a speaking voice is very essential for actors and public speakers. In daily conversation this is usually not a problem, unless those engaged in conversation are in a loud environment, such as a restaurant or a noisy pub.

1. Begin by taking long, deep breaths before you attempt to speak. Remember that long, deep breaths stretch your lung capacity. Perform this exercise by taking a deep breath, then inhaling even a bit more air. Then permit the air to release slowly out of the lungs in controlled exhalations.

2. Practice this breathing routine by saying at the same time you expand your breath, "My name is _____." Inhale deeply, and speak while gradually exhaling. Permit each word to use a bit more air then in normal conversation. Thrust more air for each word to *increase your volume*. You may utilize less air if the volume becomes too loud.

3. Attempt to speak from your diaphragm as a substitute for the lungs. It is sometimes helpful to visualize that your words are emanating from your tummy area. If done properly, this technique energizes or decreases the volume of your voice.

Exercise 2: Calculating Your Own Volume

For this exercise, you need to have a location where you can be loud; if it is at all possible, going outside is best for this exercise, even if it is a bit chilly.

Remember that volume is always an essential voice attribute. There is nothing worse than being repeatedly told by others to "Speak up, please. I [we] can't hear you!"

1. Try using the following phase:

"LONDON BRIDGE IS FALLING DOWN! YES, IT IS TRUE; LONDON BRIDGE IS FALLING DOWN!"

2. Start with the word LONDON at a very low intensity. Now, with each word of the phrase, attempt to increase your volume by a small but clearly detectable degree. Take a quick pause between each word as you increase the volume.

3. Now, try saying the word **DOWN** with a high volume of intensity and work your way down to a whisper. Go from **DOWN, DOWN, DOWN, DOWN, DOWN,** and so forth to a bare whisper…

4. Now, try the following sentences by saying the *italicized* words at a whispered, soft volume and the **bolded** words at a very loud volume. All other words should be at your natural speaking volume.

   A. I will **adjust** my *volume* to *always* be heard!
   B. **But,** can *you* hear **me** *now*?
   C. Please **turn up** the *volume*!
   D. *Sometimes* it is *important* to use **soft speech.**
   E. Please **tone** it **down;** you are *too loud*!
   F. *Loud* and **soft words** make a **speech** *attractive*!

Exercise 3: Adjust Rhythm and Tempo for Emphasis on Stage

Now that you are more motivated from exercises 1 and 2, think about rhythm and tempo. In short, *rhythm* is the pattern or blueprint of the sounds your words produce. *Tempo* is quite simply the swiftness or speed of your voice.

Rhythm is powerful in that in can carry meaning. When a speaker slows his or her tempo, this may emphasize or highlight certain words or ideas. Speeding up words and phrases can show excitement, enthusiasm, or even humor. Pausing for a moment can underscore major points or provide listeners with time to absorb an original or complex idea. *Pause* is also appropriate when you are about to make a transition from one point or idea to another.

1. Try saying the following sentences, first quite *slowly*, then very *quickly*, then finally in a more *even* or *balanced* manner somewhere in between. How is the meaning affected by the tempo each time?

    A. What do you mean my new goldfish simply jumped out of the bowl?
    B. Please, please, never mention her name to me again, never!
    C. Wow! I love that brand of chocolate; can we buy another box, maybe two?
    D. No, you mean to tell me she actually lost that election by ten votes?
    E. Sorry to hear they lost their new pedigree cat, they paid $1,000 for it?

2. Try saying the following sentences again, this time with the *pauses* as indicated. Notice how the effect of the meaning changes each time. When you speak, you can always choose just *when* and

where you want your pauses to be. *Pause* is vital for actors and can vastly effect the meaning of a line onstage.

A. What (*Pause*) do you mean my new goldfish simply jumped out (*Pause*) of the bowl?
B. Please, (*Pause*) please, never mention her name to me again, (*Pause*) never!
C. Wow! I love that (*Pause*) brand of chocolate; can we buy another box, (*Pause*) maybe two?
D. No, you mean to tell me (*Pause*) she actually lost that election by (*Pause*) ten votes?
E. Sorry to hear (*Pause*) they lost their pedigree cat; they paid (*Pause*) *how* much for it?

3. Try saying the following sentences one last time, but with the *pauses* where you wish to indicate them. Notice how the effect of the meaning changes each time in a new way. When you speak, you can always choose just *when* and *where* you want your pauses to be … this is a powerful communication tool.

A. What do you mean my new goldfish simply jumped out of the bowl?
B. Please, please, never mention her name to me again, never!
C. Wow! I love that brand of chocolate; can we buy another box, maybe two?
D. No, you mean to tell me she actually lost that election by ten votes?
E. Sorry to hear they lost their new pedigree cat; they paid $1,000 for it?

Exercise 4: Always Pitching the Right Pitch

Pitch is the frequency of the sound waves you produce when you speak onstage, in a formal public setting, or simply in a conversation you may be having in a restaurant or sports pub. Pitch is quite musical in many ways. Pitch involves being aware of properly hitting the high or low notes with your voice in a way that is most effective in communicating with your listeners. Vary your pitch throughout your presentations to establish and reinforce your message.

To avoid being monotonous, you should contrast your pitch throughout the duration of what you have to say. Pitch is powerful in that it can establish and *reinforce* your message. Pitch is very important in the art of homiletics or preaching, when giving a speech in general, and when reading in public. For actors, adjusting pitch helps create an attention-grabbing and richly rounded character.

1. Try saying the following sentences three times each at your *natural pitch* range for your voice, first quite *slowly*, then very *quickly*, then finally in a more *even* or *balanced* manner somewhere in between.

   A. Do you have a match? I need a light.
   B. Please, come here and shake my hand.
   C. Can you please lend her your book?
   D. I like matinees more than evening films.
   E. Don't forget your umbrella before you leave.
   F. Do like to watch evening sunsets or morning sunrises?

2. Try saying the following sentences three times each at your *optimum pitch*—namely, as loud as you can get without shouting! As before, begin quite *slowly*, then very *quickly*, then finally in a more *even* or *balanced* manner somewhere in between.

   A. Do you have any time for me after work tonight?
   B. Please, come here and shake my hand, or at least give me a hug.
   C. Can you please lend her your extra book? She seems lost without it in class.

D. I like matinees more than evening films, but a baseball game at night is perfect.

E. Don't forget your umbrella before you leave; last time you left your hat.

F. Do you like to watch evening sunsets or morning sunrises, or do you only watch TV?

3. Try saying the following sentences two times each, first, very *softly*, then at your *normal* or *natural* level of pitch. What effect do you think speaking softly might have on your listeners as opposed to using your more normal volume of speech?

A. Now you really know what this means, to be married.

B. Please, come here and shake the queen's hand; she's waiting.

C. Lend her your book, and chances are you'll never see it again.

D. We all like matinees more than evening films; it keeps the day younger.

E. Don't forget your umbrella before you leave; I will not return it if you do.

LISTENING INTENTLY …
Get It Correct from the Get-Go

Remember how you loved watching cartoons as a kid (maybe you still do)? If it's been a while, take a brief moment to select and watch a popular cartoon TV show for a few minutes. *Cartoon Network* shows them around the clock (and, of course, most are available online as well), so you don't have to wait for Saturday mornings anymore. But, this time, focus *not* on the images, but the *sounds* of the voices you hear. Notice how they are wonderfully rich, animated, and full of expressiveness. This high level of vocal fluency is an essential element of cartoon animations. The voices must be highly bright, full of expression, and captivating to keep children (and some of us adults as well) engaged and interested from moment to moment.

As you listen to your selected cartoon program, *close your eyes* and use your imagination. Observe how *paralanguage* is central to cartoon voices. Notice how male voices and female voices are clearly delineated by *pitch*, *rate*, and *stress*. Notice further how foreign accents (if any), animal voices, and even nonspeech background sounds wonderfully help supplement the cartoon personalities themselves. Cartoons are highly expressive (in any language) and are all about the *simplicity* of communication and the transmission of clear emotions.

The basic expressiveness of cartoons is also what competent actors and public speakers need to keep their listening audiences highly engaged, just as cartoons may do for children. Like cartoon characters, human voices must have a defined intonation. *Intonation* is the pattern of constant pitch changes that smoothly join together in a person's voice. Sometimes this is referred to as the "personal song" of an individual's voice.

It is vital that you use appropriate *intonation* when you speak; otherwise, you may be sending messages that confuse, cause doubt, or contradict what you want your words and sentences to do. As you may notice when listening to cartoons, there is no ambiguity. Everything is very apparent so that children can quickly comprehend *what*, *when*, and *where* a character is speaking and undoubtedly what it means.

F.   Evening sunsets or morning sunrises—either way the experience is divine.

Exercise 5: Controlling the Uniqueness of Your Vocal Timbre

Timbre (pronounced "*tam*-ber") is the emotional or arousing quality you release from your voice. Everyone has their own unique timbre. It is timbre that allows you to identify someone's voice on the telephone.

Timbre may also be understood as the attitude behind the words or phrases

that are spoken in your private or public speech. All listeners immediately discern a speaker's attitude and use this discernment to put meaning and understanding to what a speaker is attempting to communicate.

Always use timbre to increase meaning for your listeners and to express the emotion or attitude you desire to create. You should also select words and phrases that support the attitude you want to suggest.

Vary your natural emotional expression to support and signify meaning. Your timbre is one of the many tools with which you communicate. Practice managing your voice emotionally with the following exercises.

1. Vary your emotional expression to support and signify the designated timbre for the following sentences.

    Are you crazy? Of course I didn't tell her what happened! (as if nervous)

    Are you crazy? Of course I didn't tell her what happened! (as if confused)

    Are you crazy? Of course I didn't tell her what happened! (as if angry)

    Are you crazy? Of course I didn't tell her what happened! (as if worried)

    Are you crazy? Of course I didn't tell her what happened! (as if confident)

    Are you crazy? Of course I didn't tell her what happened! (as if in a hurry)

    Are you crazy? Of course I didn't tell her what happened! (as if afraid)

    Are you crazy? Of course I didn't tell her what happened! (as if unsure)

2. Try saying the following welcome monologue as if you are *truly sincere*. Then try it all over again, as if you really *don't* mean it at

all, but you are required to say these words, and if you do not, you will be in trouble—so you do it.

Thank you, each and every one of you, for visiting us here tonight.

We appreciate both your moral and your financial support.

You are always welcome here at our new theatre. At any time.

Oh, and if you are ever in town again, and need a place to stay for a couple of days?

Please feel free to ask any one of us in the acting company here before you leave today.

You are always welcome at each of our homes, and at *any time*.

Simply e-mail us. Or, better yet, give us a call. Our house is your house.

We love to have boarders in our homes. So, feel free to stay with us.

Exercise 6: Using Conscious Pauses as a Form of Vocal Punctuation as a Public Speaker

When speaking during a private conversation or in a public setting, a *pause* can be a very useful tool onstage. Pauses can be used to help establish clarity, emphasis, meaning, reflection, focus, attention, change of mood, or even a change in ideas. Pauses are in many ways a form of "vocal punctuation." They also help regulate the taking of turns in both interviews and in daily conversation.

On a more practical note, pausing should be frequent enough to help you catch your own breath, and, in turn, also help you regulate your rate of speech, so as not to rush what you have to say. And by not rushing your words, you will tend not to generate a sense of nervousness in your voice.

1. Try saying the following sentences with various pauses, as indicated by {p}. Think about how the meaning changes depending on when and where you pause.

   A. My favorite TV show is {p} _____.
   B. My favorite {p} TV {p} show {p} is {p} _____.
   C. My {p} favorite TV show is {p} _____.
   D. My favorite TV {p} show is {p} _____.
   E. My {p} favorite TV {p} show is {p} _____.
   F. My favorite {p} TV show is {p} _____.

2. Read the famous "Sonnet XVIII" by William Shakespeare (shown below) by inserting the pauses designated {p} as marked. Now, reread it aloud without the marked pauses, and insert pauses where you feel they should be. How has the meaning changed? Notice how your pause can control how the listener receives the poem.

   Sonnet XVIII by William Shakespeare

   Shall I compare {p} thee to a summer's {p} day?
   Thou art more lovely {p} and {p} more temperate.
   Rough winds do shake {p} the darling buds of {p} May,
   And summer's {p} lease hath all too short {p} a date.
   Sometime too hot the eye of heaven {p} shines,
   And often is his gold {p} complexion dimmed;
   And every fair {p} from {p} fair sometime declines,
   By chance, {p} or nature's changing course untrimmed;
   But thy {p} eternal summer shall not fade,
   Nor lose possession of that fair thou {p} ow'st;
   Nor shall {p} death brag thou wander'st in his shade,
   When in eternal lines {p} to Time thou grow'st.
   So long as men can {p} breathe, or eyes can {p} see,
   So long lives {p} this, and this {p} gives life to thee.

3. Improvisation exercise: Using your cell phone (while turned off), imagine that you are having a conversation with your

phone company about an incorrect bill they sent you; they are demanding immediate payment, or they will terminate your service immediately. The bill is in excess of $1,000.

They are convinced that you made the calls and will not accept that this is perhaps a serious mistake on their part. Be sure to give the impression that someone else is on the other side of the conversation by your frequent and irregular *pauses*. This is a great exercise for actors and public speakers.

Exercise 7: Using Operation to Create Emphasis

When we stress a word or sentence, we in turn are creating a focus by enforcing loudness, softness, or simply an emotional emphasis. By *stressing*, we create a sense of significance, caution, or importance. Nouns followed  by verbs are the most commonly stressed parts of speech. We point to the relative importance of a sentence or a specific part of speech by accenting a given word or short phrase; this is called *word operation*. If you have a sentence with, say, seven words in it, you have the possibility of saying it at least seven different ways by choosing to *operate* each of the words differently each time.

We point to the relative importance of a sentence or a specific part of speech by *operating* it by consciously becoming loud when we want to focus on its significance. Sometimes even stressing a simple, definite article, such as the word "the" can make a big difference in creating emphasis—as in the phrase "She was *the* best debater, bar none!"

1. Each of the following interrogative sentences has only four words. Try saying each sentence four different times by *operating* each of

the words in succession. Notice how each word, when operated separately, can vastly change the meaning of the entire sentence!

A. _Do_ you love me? Do _you_ love me? Do you _love_ me? Do you love _me_?

B. _What_ is her name? What _is_ her name? What is _her_ name? What is her _name_?

C. _He_ told you what? He _told_ you what? He told _you_ what? He told you _what_?

D. _How_ can I go? How _can_ I go? How can _I_ go? How can I _go_?

E. _Can_ I go, too? Can _I_ go, too? Can I _go_, too? Can I go, _too_?

2. Each of the following _interrogative_ sentences can be made to be _declarative_. Try saying each sentence four different times by _operating_ the punctuation. Make each interrogative sentence a declarative one.

A. Now is the time for all brave warriors to take up and give to charity?

B. She thinks she can win by losing another friend?

C. This is the day when we are to all be celebrating independence?

D. Where and just when is always the most important question?

E. Please, leave me alone; I really need to study for my exam?

What Do You Think?
Discussion Questions

1. Have you ever noticed that when people ask questions, they always end on a _higher_ note? On the other hand, affirmative statements seem to always end on a more level or slightly _lower_ pitch. Why do you think this is so? Do

you think that speakers of every language do this, not just in English?

2. What do you think might be the reverse effect of ending affirmative statements on a high pitch, and ending questions on a lower pitch?

3. Why do you think that paralanguage in some ways may be more revealing or perhaps "truthful" than the actual words or text you may perform or read before a live audience?

4. What effect do you think the loudness or softness of a phrase or even long text may have on how it is received by listeners?

Exercise 8: Oral Interpretation or Reading in Public with Eloquence

Oral interpretation (or reading in public) is the eloquent expression of presenting a poem, short story, letter, sacred scripture, or excerpt from a piece of literature before a live audience. The purpose of the oral interpreter is to establish himself or herself as a link between the author(s) of the work to be presented, and the audience who receives it in a public setting.

The essential objective of the oral interpreter should be (as best as is possible) to convey the author's intentional objectives. This often may be achieved through an exploration of the author's biography and personal perspective, along with the point in time and the circumstances under which the selection was written.

1. Bring a simple children's book to class, perhaps something from the *Cat in the Hat* series by Dr. Seuss. Now attempt to put all of your learned skills in this chapter to make it an interesting and powerful (as well as fun) experience for your listeners.

2. Write a silly poem using the following parts of speech, then read it to the class using *word operation, pitch, timbre*, and so on from this chapter. You must use all these words as given, plus you may add several of your own to the mix. Be sure to underline

the words or phrases that are required, and then _operate_ them vocally as your recite your poem.

<u>Nouns</u>: Antarctica, chewing gum, CNN, tennis, cherry ice cream, last days of Earth, clouds, Kleenex, Michael Jackson, coffee, and donuts <u>Verbs</u>: ambling, dancing, crying, to smell, limping, whispering, tickling, burped, to creep up, teasing, waiting, stirring with cheese

ABCs to Remember …

<u>A</u>ttention to the way in which you use your natural voice is more important than any script you may perform onstage in a play, any speech you may make behind a podium and microphone before an audience, or the actual words you may use during a formal or informal interview. The human voice is quite dynamic. This means that by your voice alone, you can be piercing, strident, soft, yielding, sighing, or screeching. As an actor, a public speaker, or simply a conversationalist, you have the potential to assert, proclaim, allege, declare, and even persuade.

<u>B</u>e aware that paralanguage is the audible constituents that accompany speech, which in turn _decrease_ or _increase_ the meanings of words and sentences. Paralanguage includes your _pitch_ and _volume_ and, in most cases, the _inflection_ and _intentionality_ of what you have to say.

<u>C</u>onsciously be aware of the resonance of your voice. From your voice alone, your listeners will make conclusions about your way of thinking about them and the thoughts you are

hoping to present. Through the resonance of your voice, your listeners will be able to judge your *authenticity, sincerity,* and *credibility.* In short, your voice will directly *or* indirectly shape how your listeners will act in response to you and your words, irrespective of what you say.

Don't forget that when you are *monotonous*, it puts forward to your listeners that you have little invested in them or in your message. It says to them that perhaps you really do not care very much about what they may think or feel or how they may choose to respond.

Expressive or *eloquent voices* always take the time to pause, change speed, control pacing, lower or raise volume, and regularly vary in pitch. An expressive voice is always interested in conveying sentiment, emotion, and passion.

Five Bits of JARGON to Keep Your Eyes On …

1. *Paralanguage*: The audible constituents that accompany speech and in turn decrease or increase the meanings of words and sentences. Paralanguage includes the *pitch, volume*, and, in most cases, *inflection* and *intentionality* of speech. Paralanguage is not about what you say but *how* you say it.
2. *Resonance*: The magnification and adjustment of the sound of your voice by an air-filled chamber or *cavity* of your body, such as your chest, throat, mouth, or nasal cavity. Furthermore, by the very resonance of your voice alone, your listeners will be able to judge your *authenticity, sincerity,* and *credibility.*
3. *Intonation*: The pattern of constant pitch changes that smoothly join together in a person's voice. Sometimes this is referred to as the "melody" of an individual's voice. It is vital that you use appropriate intonation when you speak,

otherwise you may be sending messages that confuse, cause doubt, or contradict what you want your words and sentences to do.

4. *Timbre*: The natural emotional quality you release from your voice. It is unique to each individual and marks your speaking voice as being distinctly you.

5. *Oral Interpretation*: The art of reading a text in public. This includes poems, letters, children's stories and even sacred texts in a house of worship.

Adjectives/Adverbs: awkwardly, gingerly, without cause, confusingly, with a sense of tipsiness, without a bit of red pepper, judgingly, brilliant

Exclamations/Questions: Wow! Not then? Oh, oh, ah! Cleo did what? Why, of course! You've got to be kidding! No way, José

Photo Credits

Headset Symbol: Copyright © 2012 Depositphotos/Tribaliumivanka.

Accessories-calculator: http://commons.wikimedia.org/wiki/File:Accessories-calculator.png.

Metronome: http://commons.wikimedia.org/wiki/File:Metronome.svg. Copyright in the Public Domain.

Montgomery Biscuits minor league baseball (affiliate of Tampa Bay Rays) pitcher #34 Jacob Thompson: Copyright © ErinNik (CC BY-SA 3.0) at http://commons.wikimedia.org/wiki/File:Montgomery-biscuits-minor-league-baseball-pitcher-34-Jacob-Thompson.jpg.

Einfacher Achtelnoten-Beat: http://commons.wikimedia.org/wiki/File:Achtelwissen_unfundiert.jpg. Copyright in the Public Domain.

Seamless Sign Pattern: Copyright © 2010 Depositphotos/Ihor Patsay.

Speech: Copyright © 2011 Depositphotos/pablonis.

Human Head with Question Mark Symbol: Copyright © 2013 Depositphotos/Pio3.

Open Book: http://commons.wikimedia.org/wiki/File:Open_book_nae_02.svg. Copyright in the Public Domain.

Ancient Greek Style: Copyright © 2011 Depositphotos/AlexTois.

Nonverbal Communication

By Amy S. E. Hubbard and Judee K. Burgoon

A s the King and his suite neared Akasaka, the palace of the Emperor, a bugle announced their arrival. The Emperor Meiji of Japan stood alone in a room adjacent to the entrance of the palace. He was dressed in European military uniform and the crest of his coat was decorated with orders. As [King] Kalakaua left the carriage and entered the palace, he stepped up to the Emperor alone and extended his arm to shake hands. For the first time in Japanese history an Emperor exchanged handshakes with a foreign sovereign (Ogawa, 1973, p. 91).

Instead of the traditional bow, this momentous meeting between two monarchs in 1881 began with a simple handshake, which served as a precursor to friendly international relations between Japan and Hawaii. More recently, the offering or withholding of a handshake between Middle Eastern leaders, reflected in this seemingly inconsequential greeting ritual, the status of peace negotiations.

So, too, are the warp and weave of daily interactions fashioned from a thousand and often presumably insignificant nonverbal gestures. A gaze broken too soon, a forced smile, a flat voice, an unreturned phone call, a conversation conducted across the barrier of an executive desk—together, such nonverbal strands form the fabric of our communicative world, defining our interpersonal relationships, declaring our personal identities, revealing our emotions, governing the flow of our social encounters, and reinforcing our attempts to influence others. Understanding human communication requires understanding the multiple nonverbal codes by which it is transacted and the communicative functions those codes accomplish.

Theorizing About Nonverbal Communication

By nonverbal communication we mean behaviors that are typically sent with intent, are used with regularity among members of a social community, are typically interpreted as intentional, and have consensually recognizable interpretations (Burgoon, Guerrero, & Floyd, in press; Bur-goon & Hoobler, 2002). This message orientation approach to communication requires attending to the meanings associated with nonverbal behaviors and focusing on meanings that are tied to communication functions within a given speech community.

Theorizing about nonverbal communication has been complicated not only by its multimodal and multifunctional nature, but also because our knowledge emanates from disparate disciplines with differing assumptions and methodologies. This makes efforts to synthesize theories and principles from all these different sources a challenge. For example, ethologists, who are interested in nonverbal communication as a basis for comparing humans to other species, approach nonverbal displays as biologically grounded signals with evolutionary survival value. Their methods require meticulous observations of nonverbal behaviors in their natural environs. Anthropologists, who see nonverbal behavior as manifestations of culture, are interested in how nonverbal rituals and norms reveal something about human society. They may rely on informants—members of a given culture—to clarify the nonverbal rules, norms, and sanctions in a given culture, or they may rely on ethnographic observations. Psychologists may examine nonverbal cues for what they reveal about intrapsychic processes such as arousal, personality, or cognition formation and processing. Among the methods used are experimental manipulations of conditions that elicit nonverbal cues or manipulations of the cues themselves. Sociologists may examine nonverbal patterns as manifestations of social hierarchies or as means toward achieving group influence and may combine observational and experimental procedures with survey methodologies. Scholars studying families, social ills, psychiatric problems, medical interactions, legal proceedings, intercultural and international relations, political image-making, and mediated versus nonmediated channels, among others, bring additional distinctive perspectives and methods to the study of nonverbal communication. Feminist scholars may address the extent to which nonverbal behaviors are tightly linked to gender and gender inequities. Computer vision experts may seek understanding of the structures and functions of nonverbal behavior to aid automated detection of human action from video. Out of all these perspectives have emerged numerous theories and models of human communication.

Obviously, no single chapter can begin to do justice to this cornucopia of nonverbal literature. We will therefore focus our attention here on a single communication function—relational communication and relationship management—and the theorizing and methods attending it. Readers interested in more broad-based reviews of nonverbal theories are directed to Burgoon and Hoobler (2002), Knapp and Hall (2006), and Manusov and Patterson (2006). Readers interested in more broad-based reviews of nonverbal measures, coding, and methodologies are directed to collections by Harrigan, Rosenthal, and Scherer (2005) and Manusov (2005).

Relational Communication and Relationship Management

Aside from emotional expression, perhaps no area has been so closely aligned with nonverbal communication as relational communication. The term *relational communication* refers *to the messages* people *exchange that define the nature of their interpersonal relationship;*

more specifically, how two people feel about one another, about their relationship, or about themselves within the context of the relationship. Relational communication undergirds all interpersonal relationships. As the coinage by which people "transact" their relationships, it purchases relational trajectories of greater or lesser intimacy, trust, interdependence, commitment, and satisfaction.

Studying relational communication requires acknowledging several important features of this major communicative function. First, relational communication takes a participant perspective. This means that people's evaluations and self-images are tied to reactions to and influenced by feedback from particular others. Second, relational communication is directed toward a specific target and not toward a generalized audience. Third, relational communication spotlights the interaction between two people, where the central unit of analysis is the *dyad*. Finally, relational communication concentrates on the meanings ascribed to the behaviors of others, rather than on the behaviors that cause certain outcomes.

Beginning with Watzlawick, Beavin, and Jackson's (1967) classic work, *Pragmatics of Human Communication,* relational communication has often been treated as synonymous with nonverbal communication. According to Watzlawick et al., all communication entails two levels, the *content* or report level (the ostensive topic of conversation) and the *relational* or command level (the definition of the interpersonal relationship which serves as a metacommunication about how to interpret the content level). In reality, not all nonverbal communication is relational, nor is all relational communication nonverbal (Bavelas, 1990), but it is evident that there is a strong division of labor such that much relational "business" is handled by the nonverbal codes while the occasioned discourse is being managed by the verbal code.

Relational Communication Dimensions

Traditional approaches to relational communication originally proposed two or three dimensions—such as control, dominance, intimacy, or inclusion—that underlie all relationships (e.g., Mehrabian,

Several exemplars illustrate how research has addressed relationship management from a nonverbal communication perspective. Detailed analyses of courtship stages and rituals have distinguished courtship cues from flirting behaviors and have revealed that different nonverbal behaviors are connected with each courtship stage (e.g., Givens, 1983; Simpson, Gangestad, & Biek, 1993). Work on relationship stages and types has identified variations in nonverbal intimacy, involvement, pleasantness, play, privacy, and emotional expressivity across such diverse relationships as acquaintance, friend, romantic, superior-subordinate, parent-child, and doctor-patient (Baxter, 1992; Guerrero & Andersen, 1991; Koerner & Fitzpatrick, 2002; Le Poire, Shepard, & Duggan, 1999; Planalp & Benson, 1992; Wagner & Smith, 1991). Other research on relationship phases has developed typologies of strategies and tactics, composed of verbal and nonverbal behaviors, used during relational escalation, maintenance, and deescalation (e.g., Cupach & Metts, 1986; Shea & Pearson, 1986; Tolhuizen, 1989). Studies of marital conflict have uncovered nonverbal profiles accompanying different conflict strategies and have shown that conflicts often take the form of reciprocal escalating spirals of nonverbal hostility with nonverbal expressions of affect playing a deciding factor in whether or not conflicts are resolved (e.g., Gottman, 1994; Newton & Burgoon, 1990; Sillars, Coletti, Parry, & Rogers, 1982). Work on relational satisfaction has identified which conflict resolution strategies and relational message themes influence satisfaction in physician–patient and marital relationships (e.g., Kelley & Burgoon, 1991; Rusbult, Verette, Whitney, Slovik, & Lipkus, 1991). Research that compares satisfied and dissatisfied couples indicates that dissatisfied couples are prone to misinterpret each other's nonverbal signals; that people in less satisfying relationships decode their partners' negative behaviors as more intentional, stable, and controllable and their partners' positive behaviors as external, unstable, and specific, whereas people in more satisfying relationships decode negative cues neutrally and positive cues as internal, stable, and global (Manusov, 1990; Noller & Ruzzene, 1991). One important conclusion is that nonverbal behaviors play a significant role in the life of a relationship by revealing its level of intimacy and closeness, distinguishing different stages or types of relationships, and affecting relational trajectories and outcomes.

Research Methods in Studying
Nonverbal Relational Communication

Our discussion of the findings in the area of nonverbal relational communication naturally brings us to consider the methods used to conduct nonverbal research on relational communication and relationship management. The methods selected affect the validity and generalizability of the conclusions that can be drawn.

A basic decision point is whether to employ an experimental or nonexperimental design and attendant measurement strategies. This is dictated by the questions and issues at stake. Often, relational communication issues require a longitudinal focus and the need to access highly private information. In such cases, researchers may incorporate nonexperimental diary and account methods. But such methodologies are fraught with the difficulties attending the use of self-report methods. For instance, respondents may be unable to provide information regarding microlevel nonverbal behaviors. It is unreasonable to expect that people are able to report all of their nonverbal behaviors (i.e., kinesics, vocalic, physical appearance, proxemic, artifactual, chronemic, and haptic cues) or that nonverbal communication occurs at a high level of awareness. Jones's (1991) examination of the problem of validity in questionnaire studies using Jourard's tactile body-accessibility scale is illustrative. It revealed that people's recall of touch behaviors was heavily influenced by expectations about which touches should have occurred; it did not match the amount of touch. This suggests that researchers must find other ways, besides exclusive reliance on self-report data, to investigate specific nonverbal behaviors, and they must have alternate means to record nonverbal behaviors without solely relying on actual participants as the primary informants.

However, if researchers are interested in the general nonverbal encoding and decoding abilities of people (e.g., to investigate what messages people intend to send, what messages people receive, and what messages people think were intentionally sent), then questionnaire measures may be a useful method of assessment. Researchers can use a number of standardized scales which have been developed to test these nonverbal skills. These scales range from self-report questionnaires to videotape tests. A variety of measures can be found in Harrigan, Rosenthal, and Scherer's (2005) *The New Handbook of Methods in Nonverbal Behavior Research* and Manusov's (2005) *The Sourcebook of Nonverbal Measures: Going Beyond Words.*

More often than not, research on nonverbal behavior entails direct observation and coding of behavior. This may occur in nonexperimental or experimental settings. In the former case, one might ask couples to interact naturally about some topic or even to recreate a previous discussion. The kinds of interaction patterns that are exhibited are then observed and coded or rated (e.g., Burman, Margolin, & John, 1993; Gottman, 1996). In the latter case, some interactants might experimentally alter some behaviors—perhaps becoming uninvolved and detached—to see the effects on partner behavior or interpretations or on observer interpretations (e.g., Guerrero & Burgoon, 1996). Or couples might be placed under different experimental conditions, such as conducting a joint task and discussing personal fears, and their behavior patterns compared across partners and conditions (e.g., Newton & Burgoon, 1990). Although nonverbal behaviors may be observed live or "online," researchers interested in nonverbal cues often analyze a permanent record of the interaction. Nonverbal studies typically use audiotapes, videotapes, or digital recordings, depending on the specific research questions, and the ease and availability of using particular recording devices. Once they are recorded, nonverbal behaviors are frequently coded by outside observers. This is in line with a message orientation approach. In addition, in the case of relational communication, participants may also report their perceptions. One consequence of conducting nonverbal research in this manner is the additional expenses—in time and money—associated with equipment costs, hiring coders, training coders, and altering the digital recordings, videotapes, or audiotapes to aid in coding (e.g., content-filtering procedures). Another consequence is that interpretation of the non-verbal data may become more difficult as various perspectives are taken into account. In the case where both participants and outside observers judge the nonverbal behaviors recorded, there may be striking differences in their ratings. For example, various research programs comparing participant and trained observer perspectives showed that observers and participants share some commonalities in perceptions but also some notable discrepancies (e.g., Burgoon & Newton, 1991; Floyd & Markman, 1983; Rusbult et al., 1991).

A final important consideration when conducting nonverbal research is the unit of analysis. Will it consist of nonverbal measurement of single and concrete behaviors, where observation is usually event-based or time-based using small time intervals (micro level) or nonverbal measurement of larger and more abstract behaviors, where observation is usually time-based using larger time intervals or event-based using larger events (macro level)? Burgoon and Baesler (1991) suggested that nonverbal researchers should: (1) assess the representational validity between the level of measurement and the nonverbal phenomena of conceptual interest, such that the unit of measurement is socially meaningful; (2) compare the reliability using different levels of measurement; (3) consider the concurrent validity between the micro and macro measures; and (4) measure the predictive power using micro and macro measurements when determining the appropriate measurement strategy for particular research questions.

Conclusion

Understanding nonverbal communication entails recognition that research and theorizing in this field is based on a diverse foundation of interests. In this [chapter], we sampled the vast array of approaches and methods for studying nonverbal communication to better appreciate the richness and complexity of research in this area. We gave special attention to the communicative function of relational communication, demonstrating how nonverbal scholars have sought to understand relationships through people's nonverbal behavior. In addition, we examined important decision points for those interested in research methods used in the study of nonverbal communication. Finally, we discussed a specific sample experiment to demonstrate how one might conduct a study on the nonverbal aspects of relational conflicts.

Other areas likely to attract increasing research attention are significant nonverbal events in relationships that affect the direction of a relationship's development, infrequent nonverbal events, and expected but omitted nonverbal cues as relational statements. For instance, the first time you and a potential romantic partner hold hands may signal an escalation in the relationship, or the one time that you yell and slam your fist into the wall during a conflict may signal a downward trend in your relationship. The absence of a goodbye kiss may be more telling to a spouse about the intimacy of the marriage than any other cue present. Nonverbal behaviors that are rarely performed or intermittent behaviors are likely to receive more attention as researchers try to find ways of capturing or observing them. Also, descriptions of the frequency and duration of specific relational cues, their sequences and cycles over time, the interrelatedness among cues, and changes in relational meaning depending on their placement in the relational trajectory are choice areas of investigation. The previous overemphasis on single cue and static analyses will surely give way to analyzing the interplay among multiple cues, longitudinal patterns, and the impact of those patterns on relational outcomes such as commitment and satisfaction.

As we explore these areas of study, we must recognize that answers to our questions may come from a diverse set of literatures and a variety of scholarly fields. Integration of research and theorizing on nonverbal communication can only aid in our search to better understand our nonverbal communication. Nonverbal researchers have only begun to tap this rich area of study as they strive to fully depict the role of nonverbal communication in the process of relationship communication and management.

References

Bavelas, J. B. (1990). Behaving and communicating: A reply to Motley. *Western Journal of Speech Communication, 54,* 593–602.

Baxter, L. A. (1992). Forms and functions of intimate play in personal relationships. *Human Communication Research, 18,* 336–363.

Burgoon, J. K. (1991). Relational message interpretations of touch, conversational distance, and posture. *Journal of Nonverbal Behavior, 15,* 233–259.

Burgoon, J. K., & Baesler, E. J. (1991). Choosing between micro and macro nonverbal measurement: Application to selected vocalic and kinesic indices. *Journal of Nonverbal Behavior, 15,* 57–78.

Burgoon, J. K., & Dunbar, N. E. (2005). Nonverbal expressions of dominance and power in human relationships. In V. Manusov & M. L. Patterson (Eds.), *The Sage handbook of nonverbal communication* (pp. 279–298). Thousand Oaks, CA: Sage.

Burgoon, J. K., Guerrero, L. G., & Floyd, K. (in press). *Nonverbal communication.* Boston, MA: Allyn & Bacon.

Burgoon, J. K., & Hale, J. L. (1984). The fundamental topoi of relational communication. *Communication Monographs, 51,* 193–214.

Burgoon, J. K., & Hale, J. L. (1987). Validation and measurement of the fundamental themes of relational communication. *Communication Monographs, 54,* 19–41.

Burgoon, J. K., & Hoobler, G. D. (2002). Nonverbal signals. In M. L. Knapp & G. R. Miller (Eds.), *Handbook of interpersonal communication* (3rd ed., pp. 240–299). Thousand Oaks, CA: Sage.

Burgoon, J. K., & Newton, D. A. (1991). Applying a social meaning model to relational messages of conversational involvement: Comparing participant and observer perspectives. *Southern Communication Journal, 56,* 96–113.

Burman, B., Margolin, G., & John, R. S. (1993). America's angriest home videos: Behavioral contingencies observed in home reenactments of marital conflict. *Journal of Consulting and Clinical Psychology, 61,* 28–39.

Cappella, J. N. (1994). The management of conversational interaction in adults and infants. In M. L. Knapp & G. R. Miller (Eds.), *Handbook of interpersonal communication* (2nd ed., pp. 380–418). Thousand Oaks, CA: Sage.

Coker, D. A., & Burgoon, J. K. (1987). The nature of conversational involvement and nonverbal encoding patterns. *Human Communication Research, 13*, 463–494.

Cupach, W. R., & Metts, S. (1986). Accounts of relational dissolution. *Communication Monographs, 53*, 311–334.

Dillard, J. P., Solomon, D. H., & Palmer, M. T. (1999). Structuring the concept of relational communication. *Communication Monographs, 66*, 49–65.

Dunbar, N. E., & Burgoon, J. K. (2005a). Nonverbal measurement of dominance. In V. Manusov (Ed.), *The sourcebook of nonverbal measures: Going beyond words* (pp. 361–374). Hillsdale, NJ: Erlbaum.

Dunbar, N. E., & Burgoon, J. K. (2005b). Perceptions of power and interactional dominance in interpersonal relationships. *Journal of Social and Personal Relationships, 22*, 207–233

Floyd, F. J., & Markman, H. J. (1983). Observational biases in spouse observation: Toward a cognitive/behavioral model of marriage. *Journal of Consulting and Clinical Psychology, 51*, 450–457.

Givens, D. B. (1983). *Love signals*. New York, NY: Crown.

Gottman, J. M. (1994). *What predicts divorce? The relationship between marital processes and marital outcomes*. Mahwah, NJ: Erlbaum.

Gottman, J. M. (1996). *What predicts divorce? The measures*. Mahwah, NJ: Erlbaum.

Guerrero, L. K., & Andersen, P. A. (1991). The waxing and waning of relational intimacy: Touch as a function of relational stage, gender, and touch avoidance. *Journal of Social and Personal Relationships, 8*, 147–165.

Guerrero, L. K., & Burgoon, J. K. (1996). Attachment styles and reactions to nonverbal involvement change in romantic dyads: Patterns of reciprocity and compensation. *Human Communication Research, 22*, 335–370.

Hall, J. A. (2006). Nonverbal behavior, status, and gender: How do we understand their relations? *Psychology of Women Quarterly, 30*, 384–391.

Harrigan, J. A., Rosenthal, R., & Scherer, K. R. (Eds.). (2005). *The new handbook of methods in nonverbal behavior research*. New York, NY: Oxford University Press.

Hendrick, S., & Hendrick, C. (1992). *Liking, loving, & relating* (2nd ed.). Pacific Grove, CA: Brooks/Cole.

Jones, S. E. (1991). Problems of validity in questionnaire studies of nonverbal behavior: Jourard's Tactile Body-Accessibility Scale. *Southern Communication Journal, 56,* 83–95.

Jourard, S. M. (1966). An exploratory study of body-accessibility. *British Journal of Social and Clinical Psychology, 5,* 221–231.

Kelley, D. L., & Burgoon, J. K. (1991). Understanding marital satisfaction and couple type as functions of relational expectations. *Human Communication Research, 18,* 40–69.

Knapp, M. L., & Hall, J. A. (2006). *Nonverbal communication in human interaction* (6th ed.). Toronto, Canada: Thomson Wadsworth.

Koerner, A. F., & Fitzpatrick, M. A. (2002). Nonverbal communication and marital adjustment and satisfaction: The role of decoding relationship relevant and relationship irrelevant affect. *Communication Monographs, 69,* 33–51.

Le Poire, B., & Burgoon, J. K. (1994). Two contrasting explanations of involvement violations: Expectancy violations theory versus discrepancy arousal theory. *Human Communication Research, 20,* 560–591.

Le Poire, B. A., Shepard, C., & Duggan, A. (1999). Nonverbal involvement, expressiveness, and pleasantness as predicted by parental and partner attachment style. *Communication Monographs, 66,* 293–311.

Manusov, V. (1990). An application of attribution principles to nonverbal behaviors in romantic dyads. *Communication Monographs, 57,* 104–118.

Manusov, V. (Ed.). (2005). *The sourcebook of nonverbal measures: Going beyond words.* Mahwah, NJ: Erlbaum.

Manusov, V., & Patterson, M. L. (Eds.). (2006). *The Sage handbook of nonverbal communication.* Thousand Oaks, CA: Sage.

Mehrabian, A. (1981). *Silent messages.* Belmont, CA: Wadsworth.

Newton, D. A., & Burgoon, J. K. (1990). Nonverbal conflict behaviors: Functions, strategies, and tactics. In D. D. Cahn (Ed.), *Intimates in conflict* (pp. 77–104). Hillsdale, NJ: Erlbaum.

Noller, P., & Ruzzene, M. (1991). Communication in marriage: The influence of affect and cognition. In G. J. Fletcher & F. D. Fincham (Eds.), *Cognition in close relationships* (pp. 203–233). Hillsdale, NJ: Erlbaum.

Ogawa, D. M. (1973). *Jan ken po: The world of Hawaii's Japanese Americans.* Honolulu, HI: University of Hawaii Press.

Patterson, M. L. (1983). *Nonverbal behavior: A functional perspective*. New York, NY: Springer Verlag.

Planalp, S., & Benson, A. (1992). Friends' and acquaintances' conversations I: Perceived differences. *Journal of Social and Personal Relationships, 9*, 483–506.

Register, L. M., & Henley, T. B. (1992). The phenomenology of intimacy. *Journal of Social and Personal Relationships, 9*, 467–481.

Ridgeway, C. L., Berger, J., & Smith, L. (1985). Nonverbal cues and status: An expectation states approach. *American Journal of Sociology, 90*, 955–978.

Riggio, R. E. (1986). Assessment of basic social skills. *Journal of Personality and Social Psychology, 51*, 649–660.

Rusbult, C. E., Verette, J., Whitney, G. A., Slovik, L. F., & Lipkus, I. (1991).Accommodation processes in close relationships: Theory and preliminary empirical evidence. *Journal of Personality and Social Psychology, 60*, 53–78.

Shea, B. C., & Pearson, J. C. (1986). The effects of relationship type, partner intent, and gender on the selection of relationship maintenance strategies. *Communication Monographs, 53*, 352–364.

Sillars, A. L., Coletti, S. F., Parry, D., & Rogers, M. A. (1982). Coding verbal conflict tactics: Nonverbal and perceptual correlates of the "avoidance-distributive-integrative" distinction. *Human Communication Research, 9*, 83–95.

Simpson, J. A., Gangestad, S. W., & Biek, M. (1993). *Journal of Experimental Social Psychology, 29*, 434–461.

Tolhuizen, J. H. (1989). Communication strategies for intensifying dating relationships: Identification, use and structure. *Journal of Social and Personal Relationships, 6*, 413–434.

Trimboli, A., & Walker, M. (1993). The CAST test of nonverbal sensitivity. *Journal of Language and Social Psychology, 12*, 49–65.

Wagner, H. L., & Smith, J. (1991). Facial expression in the presence of friends and strangers. *Journal of Nonverbal Behavior, 15*, 201–214.

Watzlawick, P., Beavin, J. H., & Jackson, D. D. (1967). *Pragmatics of human communication: A study of interactional patterns, pathologies, and paradoxes*. New York, NY: Norton.

Zuckerman, M., & Larrance, D. T. (1979). Individual differences in perceived encoding and decoding abilities. In R. Rosenthal (Ed.), *Skill in nonverbal communication: Individual differences* (pp. 171–203). Cambridge, MA: Oelgeschlager, Gunn, & Hain.

Give Great Presentations

By Everett Chasen and Bob Putnam

"There are always three speeches for every one you actually gave. The one you practiced, the one you gave, and the one you wish you gave."
—Dale Carnegie

In This Chapter

- Why speeches are still important.
- Look at good and bad speech examples.
- See a sample introduction and use the checklist.
- See a systematic approach to develop and deliver great oral presentations.
- Check out surefire tips to make your words both effective and dynamic.

The speech—simple delivery of the spoken word to a person or group—sometimes seems like a dinosaur in the Jurassic Park of modern communication methods.

Everett Chasen and Bob Putnam, "Give Great Presentations," The Manager's Communication Toolbox, pp. 47-50, 52-62. Copyright © 2012 by Association for Talent Development (ATD). Reprinted with permission.

Plain old voice power is ancient when compared with digital electronic transmission of information around the world at the speed of light. And it's not just sophisticated business communication that outpaces old-fashioned speech. Today's average thirteen-year-old owns communication devices of global range and light-speed capabilities: Androids and iPhones; Blackberries and iPads; Nooks and Kindles (The Pew Research Center, 2009).

But sometimes you've just got to talk to other people. Meetings still exist (although many have gone virtual); lawyers still speak to juries; politicians still reach out to voters; and there are thousands of other occasions when the personal dimension of a face-to-face discussion, a group briefing, or a full-scale speech is just what's needed to get your point across.

Like the old grey mare, though, a speech isn't what it used to be. Our world does move faster than it used to. Newspapers have pretty much lost timeliness to television, and television, in turn, has lost its timeliness to faster, more diverse information sources like Twitter, Facebook, and Skype. People who communicate with a minimum number of keystrokes today, and make decisions with an electronic nod of the head, have little patience with wordy rambling. Consider the following scenario:

A hush of anticipation falls over the audience as the speaker steps up to the lectern. He's tightly clutching a set of notes, suggesting he's got something important to say. Do those pages contain profound wisdom on the organization's direction? Has he solved the problem that's kept the company from joining the Fortune 500? Or at least, has he got something to say that will keep everyone entertained for a while?

As the air of excitement draws listeners forward on their seats to catch the speaker's opening line, his first, memorable words reverberate through the hall. "Whap..." "Whap..." "Whap..." "Is this thing on? Everyone hear me? OK, hello. Good morning, ladies and gentlemen. I'm so great to be, I mean...it's great, uh, I'm pleased to be here today."

(In fact, he doesn't look pleased to be there. He put his notes on top of the lectern, and now he's got a death grip on its sides.)

"When our program chairman, Henry Smith, called me, awhile back, and asked me to be the kickoff speaker at our annual conference, well, I was just really surprised. You know, Ol' Hank and I go back a long ways. We've been here through a number of these conferences, let me tell you. We go back to the days when our meetings were half this size, and held in the old Quonset huts—when you had to walk across the parking lot to use the Porta-Potties. Now, of course, we have this new building with the classy restrooms just inside the main entrance, but that's another story.

"Anyway, I was surprised this time, because it's a pretty big honor to speak at the plenary session, instead of just a breakout group, like I usually do. I should mention that I WILL also be giving my usual technical update during a couple of the breakout periods. You can find the times listed under tab seven in the back of the conference notebook.

But since I DO have this shot at talking to the entire group, I want to give you my take on how things are going in our field of systematic supervisory subrogation. If you'll bear with me, I've got some pretty thorough notes here, so I can give you the details concerning each of the 26 cases in adjudication."

The speaker then reads from his thick ream of notes, not bothering to look up from the technically detailed text. It's hard to decide whether his boring reading is worse than his disconnected introduction, in which he bounced from the location of restrooms to the schedule for breakout sessions.

The excitement and energy bleeds out of the room like air from a leaking balloon. A few in the audience are still listening to the speaker just to guess, "How bad can this get?" All over the room, the dim light of smartphones can be seen, as if a swarm of fireflies had suddenly been set free. Some people are thumbing through their program notebooks, trying to figure out when they'd need to return if they staged a daring escape to their rooms, the lobby, or the golf course. Others close their eyes to concentrate and pray that they do not begin to actually snore. A lucky few who remembered to bring the *USA Today* from their room pull it out to work the crossword puzzle.

Let's trace the ugly trajectory of this presentation scenario to see where it went wrong. Our example speaker gave good indication, in those initial moments, that his presentation would be pedestrian at best. The signals said that, more than likely, it was going to be crushingly, soul-numbingly boring. Communication professors and public-speaking consultants agree that an audience forms its first impressions about a speaker in a matter of seconds. This magical time window has been cited as about seven seconds (Kinsey Goman, 2011).

Fortunately for audiences around the world, most speakers are not as bad as the person in this example. But far too many of them begin with two signal failures in those vital first few seconds: to grab the audience's attention (in a positive way, of course) and to make a good first impression. Indeed, the vast majority of public speakers waste that precious initial time with dull salutations, such as, "Good morning, I'm pleased to be here ..." or something equally vapid. Why? Our guess is that this kind of introduction does serve a perceived purpose: It calms speakers down. It gives them the opportunity to hear their voice making a somewhat reassuring—although bland—sound.

How much more compelling it would have been if the speaker in our example immediately launched into a dramatic story, made an intriguing statement of fact, or asked a provocative question! Imagine if he walked to the microphone, and began:

Thirty-eight years ago today, a young man walked into a meeting at this very location, wearing the uniform of a U.S. Marine just released from active duty.

His uniform was wrinkled and smelled of mothballs from being stuffed into a sea bag—because he'd been wearing jungle utilities for a very long time. But he wore that uniform proudly anyway, especially the ribbons that reflected his service in the hardest-fought months of the Vietnam War.

Not everyone he'd met since returning to his country respected that uniform. Anger over the war and his country's policies had led several people to make nasty remarks as he passed by. But he'd heard there was a chance to get a job with a new organization having a meeting here—and the uniform was the only polite clothing he owned.

He smiled when he arrived and found that the meeting was being held in old Quonset buildings; the surplus military structures made him feel at home. When he walked in, the people at the new organization also made him feel at home. They understood the sense of patriotism that led him to wear his uniform. And they made it clear they respected his service and appreciated his sacrifices.

Ladies and gentlemen, I was that young marine—the guy who walked into the annual meeting of this organization, nearly four decades ago. In the years since then, I've been blessed with a good job, a lot of great co-workers, and even a few promotions along the way. I've never forgotten the way I was received here, and I've tried my best to make myself part of the accepting, supporting culture that has meant so much to me and my family. Today, I'm honored to welcome you to this plenary session of our annual meeting and to give you an update on a few key areas...

Of course, not everyone has such a heartwarming personal story to tell. And starting off dramatically doesn't always work; sometimes a more reserved style is appropriate. But most people and most organizations have moving stories to tell, and there are lots of other ways to create a lively opening for a talk.

In our first example, the speaker compounded his poor beginning by starting to read from his notes. He didn't even try to look up every once in a while to make eye contact with his audience. This is one of public speaking's worst sins; if you treat your speech as a reading exercise, you are directly inviting your audience to tune you out and turn on their smartphones. Want to avoid this pitfall? Keep in mind that every speech, presentation, and briefing is a performance. You're not turning in a term paper or submitting a report. You're trying to make a connection with the audience.

The verbal content of a speech—the actual words people say—is not the only important thing in any presentation. Experts on spoken communication generally agree that the verbal content of a speech is less important (perhaps considerably so) than how a speaker looks and sounds. This assertion caused quite a stir at a convention for corporate speechwriters, held in Chicago a few years ago. Attendees were startled when the results of a UCLA psychology study were presented to this group of professional communicators. The study postulated there are three elements in any human communication: words, vocal sound, and the nonverbal factors of appearance and physical gestures. And it concluded, based on survey data, that audience perceptions of a speech are based 55 percent on a speaker's appearance, 33 percent on the way a speaker sounds, and only 7 percent on the actual words of the speech (Mehrabian & Wiener, 1967).

You can imagine how poorly that news was received by a group of people who write speeches for a living. But the unflappable moderator, the late journalist and spokesperson Tony Snow (who was then the press secretary for President George H.W. Bush) made several shrewd observations. First, since speechwriters chronically consider themselves to be underpaid, Mr. Snow humorously opined that everyone present might wish to keep this study confidential from their employers.

Rather than waste energy arguing which elements of public speaking are most important, Snow suggested it would be best to simply emphasize to speakers that sticking to the script is not enough: their appearance and the way they sound are extremely important.

Whether presented starkly by a social scientist, or in the understated, practical manner of Tony Snow, the message is the same: A speech is a performance. How you look and how you sound are at least as important as what you say. No matter how communication technology evolves in the future, looking and sounding prepared and professional will always be the keys to avoiding mediocrity as a speaker.

The Design Blueprint or Outline

EXPERT TIP

Mary Grealy is president of the Healthcare Leadership Council (HLC), a coalition of chief executives from several disciplines in American healthcare, including hospitals, health plans, pharmaceutical companies, medical device manufacturers, and academic health centers. Grealy gets frequent requests to provide informational briefings, congressional testimony, and other forms of public commentary. Her advice for putting together effective presentations:

- **Build your talk by collecting information about the potential audience.** This will help focus your presentation. A checklist (Figure 13-1) is a helpful tool in making sure you avoid pitfalls.
- **Find out whether audiovisuals will be appropriate and supported.** Are there any special formats or requirements?
- **Even if the meeting agenda is not final when you call, press for whatever information is available.** You can find out things to help avoid surprises.
- **When you will be part of a panel, ask who the other members will be, and the order of speakers.** Suggest that the sponsoring organization set up a conference call among panelists in advance, to avoid redundancy and to make the whole presentation more coherent.
- **Send a copy of your biography or resume to the inviting organization.** Even if they don't ask for it, it's usually appreciated. Include a short, "suggested intro" for yourself. Bring an extra copy when you go to speak (introducers sometimes don't get the advance materials, and they'll be grateful!).

Figure 13-1   A Checklist for Speeches and Presentations

Here is a list of questions to answer before you start writing your presentation:

- What organization is requesting the presentation?
- What topics are they interested in, and what other subjects should be covered?
- Where and when will the presentation be given?
- How large will the audience be, and are there any people of special importance attending?
- What are key characteristics of the audience? (If relevant, include information about their average age, education level, political orientation, and the depth of their knowledge on the subject to be discussed.)
- How much time has the inviting organization allotted for the presentation?
- What is the format of the presentation? Is it a keynote address, one in a series of presentations, or a panel discussion?
- Would the organization like to have time for questions and answers?
- What is the meeting's theme? What's the rest of the agenda like? Who else is speaking, and what are the topics of their presentations?
- Who will introduce the speaker? Who is the point of contact for the organization?
- Does the organization require a copy of the prepared remarks or a speech title in advance of the presentation? If so, when?
- What are the physical details of the presentation location, including
  - What is the stage layout?
  - How will the panel be seated?
  - How large is the lectern? (Will it accommodate my notes or a laptop; does it have a light?)
  - Will a wireless microphone be available?
  - What other audiovisual support will there be?
- What other administrative details are there, including
  - How will the speaker get to the site?
  - Who is paying the speaker's expenses?
  - Is there an honorarium? If so, how much has the organization offered?

Every so often, you may be asked to make a unique kind of presentation, such as one that involves a skit or a song. But the majority of speeches, presentations, and even briefings consist of an introduction, a body of content (sometimes called the argument or evidence) and a conclusion.

Lots of people have different ideas on how to get your audience's attention at the beginning of a speech, but no one disagrees that it's absolutely vital to do so. Get the audience's attention immediately by making a provocative statement or telling a compelling story: something that will captivate them, pique their curiosity, or stimulate their interest.

Don't risk writer's block by trying to compose the exact wording of the opening during this initial outline phase. As you sketch out the rest of your presentation, and go through your research materials, you'll think of ideas for a compelling statement or moving story.

After the introduction, you may want to provide a road map, in the form of a quick preview of the things you're going to talk about. You probably don't need to do this when your talk is one in a series of panel speeches, or otherwise part of a larger presentation. But if your speech is a stand-alone presentation, the road map can help the audience follow your points more easily. Keep your preview short; spending too much time on what you intend will make the audience think you are long-winded.

The next element of your speech's blueprint is to outline the main body, or the significant points of the speech. Here's where you provide supporting ideas and details—sometimes referred to as evidence—and any examples you've developed to prove or reinforce those points. After listing the main points, the classic approach would have you provide a summary. The last item in the blueprint is the conclusion, which should project a sense of finality. So, taking a classic approach to preparing a speech outline includes

- an introduction—establishing rapport between speaker and audience
- points of evidence—presented to stimulate and convince

Figure 13-2 Sample Introduction

> On the day he was sworn in as Secretary of Veterans Affairs, Anthony Principi promised he would do his utmost to ensure that America's veterans and their families would receive all of the services and benefits they have rightfully earned from their service to our nation. It was a promise he not only kept during his four years as Secretary—but one he has kept throughout his entire life.
>
> Secretary Principi is a proud graduate of the United States Naval Academy, was a river patrol unit commander in Vietnam, and is a former member of the Navy Judge Advocate General's Corps.
>
> He served with distinction as chief counsel and staff director of the Senate Committee on Veterans Affairs; as counsel to the Senate Armed Services Committee; and as chair of both the Commission on Servicemembers and Veterans Transition Assistance and of President George W. Bush's Defense Base Closure and Realignment Committee. He also served three separate tours of duty with the Department of Veterans Affairs as assistant secretary, deputy secretary, and finally as VA secretary from 2001–2005.
>
> Secretary Principi has also been the chair of the Naval Academy's Board of Visitors; the vice president for government affairs for Pfizer, and the executive chairman of QTC Management. Ladies and gentlemen, it is my privilege to introduce to you one of the greatest friends our nation's veterans have ever had: the Honorable Anthony J. Principi.

- a summary—succinctly recounting the argument, and carrying momentum forward
- a conclusion—wrapping up in a call to action.

The Framework—Flesh Out the Words

Informed by the research you've done on the audience, and guided by your outline, now it's time to compose the words of the speech. Some speakers don't formally take this step. They rely on their knowledge and any outlining or notes they've prepared to allow them to speak more spontaneously.

If you're going to do this, you'd better be well-versed in the subject matter, have a very orderly thought process, and be exceptionally adept at word choice. But most of us will be much better off with a little more preparation.

Even those few who speak without notes will benefit from fully constructing the framework of the speech. We recommend composing the words in advance of the presentation. The process of physically writing or typing out the words—or reading and editing drafts prepared by staff—allows you to think through arguments, find the most logical approach, and smoothly present those arguments as eloquently, briefly, and understandably as possible.

Here's another reason to write out what you're going to say, even if you don't take the words to the podium with you: The process of writing and working through the words is a proven memory aid. In many instances, speakers who have written their words in advance find they can recite long passages verbatim, with little or no reference to their notes. Then, during the actual presentation, a quick glance at talking points is all they need.

Writing for smooth expression and eloquent phrasing should not be confused with using elaborate, overly complex words and unnecessary, high-flown allusions. Especially with the spoken word, clear, simple language is the best platform for ideas and evokes the strongest feelings. This phase is also the time to comb out the acronyms, abbreviations, and techie terms that populate notes during early stages of speech building. These language shortcuts are audience losers.

Fill in the Structure with Audience Stimulators

With a solid framework in place, fill in the structure by using techniques to emphasize important points, to make the talk lively, and to involve the audience. This includes selection of audiovisual materials, first-person stories, anecdotes, quotations, questions, and other rhetorical flourishes. Nonverbal behaviors also stimulate the audience, such as eye contact, facial expressions, posture and body orientation, proximity to the audience, and gestures.

Audiovisuals

Audiovisual support is a key decision for a speaker today. Technology has advanced at a startling pace for digital imagery, and audience expectations and tastes have changed to follow that trend. For many people, yesterday's question, "Can I find a few illustrations for my speech?" has become today's: "Can I find a few words to accompany my illustrations?"

Desktop presentation support programs have become so capable and complex that there are many books on each program. [Other chapters go] into more detail on which program to use and why. But videos and still images should support your presentation, not detract from it. Your goal is to find a way to deliver a successful presentation, using an effective blend of words and images.

Rhetorical Techniques

"Rhetoric" comes from ancient Greece, where it was Aristotle's favorite subject. Rhetoric describes the way public speakers move audiences to action with arguments. And a few rhetorical techniques—like simile, analogy, and metaphor—can be useful to the average speaker.

These three figures of speech, which are sometimes confused with one another, help explain complex concepts by making comparisons to other things or ideas. The most common technique is the simile. This figure of speech describes two fundamentally different things as being similar, by using the words "like" or "as." Here are some examples:

- The speaker was as sharp as a tack.
- That unexciting presentation was like watching paint dry.

Metaphors directly describe an object or idea with a known term, implying some similarity between them. A metaphor uses one thing to mean another and creates a comparative relationship between the two words.

- The stage in front of the spotlights was an oven.
- The moderator was boiling mad when my speech ran overtime.

An analogy is a comparison of certain similarities between things which are otherwise unlike:

- Writing a speech without an outline has much in common with planning a voyage without a chart.
- Giving an important speech without rehearsing your lines is the kind of gamble you take when playing an important sports game without having practiced.

The key to using rhetorical techniques is to make your points clear by putting life into your words.

Quotations

Famous quotations are as integral to public speaking as the lectern or podium at the front of the hall. In pre-Internet days, the bookshelves of any self-respecting speechwriter, as well as those of many executives, prominently featured *Bartlett's Familiar Quotations*. After all, what better way to imply the profound nature of a speaker's observations than to express them through a proverb, or the words of a famous person? The strategy can be effective. Audiences traditionally have a reverence for wisdom or humor so aptly expressed that the words have stood the test of time. And there's no shortage of material. Among the most prolifically quoted are sources so famous that only one name need be cited: Shakespeare, Franklin, Lincoln, Thoreau, Emerson, Churchill. With today's Internet search engines and old-fashioned texts filled with famous quotations, you can find an insightful or witty saying to open any talk, support any argument, and evocatively put a period at the end of any conclusion.

To make effective use of quotations, choose wisely and sparingly. Audiences may enjoy reflecting on a quote from antiquity, or from a prominent, quirky celebrity—perhaps Yogi Berra—if the saying fits the situation that's being discussed or the point that's being made. But when it's hard to relate the quote to the subject at hand, or when the speaker uses too many quotes, it's no longer a beneficial tactic.

Among professional speechwriters working in politics, there is a near-insatiable demand for quotes extolling our nation's virtues. Inevitably, the search leads virtually all of them to one particular source: Alexis de Tocqueville. As the noble experiment of democracy was born, few individuals wrote more expansively or glowingly about the majesty of America and its democratic virtues than this French observer; his fulsome words have become so overused among contemporary speechwriters that a standing joke among political scribes is, "Don't quote de Tocque."

Here's some bottom-line summary advice for using quotes: Keep it on point, keep it limited, and keep it fresh. As Mark Twain advised: "Everything has its limit; iron ore cannot be educated into gold."

The Rule of Threes

One of the most powerful techniques for bringing your words to life, as well as one of the easiest to build into your presentation, is the rule of threes. The term "rule of threes" has application in math, medicine, music, and architecture. But it is best known as a technique applied to writing and public speaking. From the earliest examples of literature (Julius Caesar's line, "Veni, Vidi, Vici"—I came, I saw, I conquered—is one of the first that has survived), writers have exhibited an understanding of the power of three.

There is a sweeping influence of the rule of threes in our language. It is a prevalent plot structure in fables, stories, and jokes. The rule of threes is found everywhere:

- religious writings (Father, Son, and Holy Spirit)
- scientific classifications (animal, vegetable, mineral)
- articulation of public policy (of the people, by the people, for the people)
- religious virtues (faith, hope, and charity)

- descriptions of what's important in our society (life, liberty, and the pursuit of happiness)
- memorable book and movie titles (*The Good, the Bad, and the Ugly* and *Sex, Lies, and Videotape*)

Listening to a speech subjects us to a flow of thoughts and ideas, challenging us to somehow organize this new information. The offer of three clearly identified points within this flow appeals to our sense of order; we're given some handholds to help us grip the meaning of the speaker's words. The rule of threes is also helpful for making gestures. Ticking off three points on your fingers is a natural way of using your hands. Any time you can articulate three points in your speech with effusive but graceful hand gestures, you will bring a sense of order to your argument in a lively way.

In writing your presentation, you may be fortunate enough to identify naturally occurring sets of three. But successful writers and speakers also find ways to create them. For example, Shakespeare wanted to write more compelling words to start Mark Antony's eulogy for Caesar than: "My friends," or "My fellow Romans." He could describe the audience as friends, and they were also Romans. Could he find a third way to describe them? How much more powerful it was to say "Friends, Romans, countrymen, lend me your ears."

In a more contemporary example, imagine a politician who wants to tell an audience that a new interstate road proposal will be good for commuters, and—because it's cost effective—also good for taxpayers. How could this speaker add another beneficiary, to facilitate the rule of threes? How about: "This proposal is good for commuters; it's good for taxpayers; it's good for America!"

If your presentation involves more than three points, strongly consider citing only three. Let's say, for instance, there are 11 challenges facing your organization, or that your division has recorded nine accomplishments. A good approach is to mention the actual number, and then call attention to just three examples. You will use the power of threes, but you'll also recognize the reality that most audiences can't assimilate a long list of points presented orally.

As useful as the rule of threes may be, it shouldn't be applied rigidly; there are instances in which two, or four, or some other number of points is so important that they shouldn't be artificially changed. Patrick Henry's famous statement included two parts that would not be improved by the addition of a third: "Give me liberty, or give me death."

Dress, Body Language, Stage Kinetics, and Paralinguistics

As discussed earlier, audience perception of a speaker depends on how the speaker looks and sounds. Appearance begins with attire—a significant factor in business communication. For the days you need to give a speech or major presentation, here are some tips.

Dark gray and dark blue suits (or sport jacket/slacks combos) are the safest bets for both men and women. White shirts and blouses may not sound exciting or fashionable, but in a hotel meeting room they're your best bet to accent a business suit, especially when seen from the back of the room. Keep your suit jacket buttoned during your presentation and you'll automatically look more businesslike. Wear it open, and you'll have a more casual look. One is not better than the other, yet you make a statement about attitude toward subject matter and audience with the option you choose.

Personal accessories, including jewelry and wristwatches, can distract your listeners if they dominate your visual presentation. If you are not sure about how your accessories will affect your audience, keep them in your pocket or briefcase until after the presentation. Avoid tinted glasses, which tend to block eye contact.

Body Language

Body language includes posture, gestures, facial expressions, and eye movement. The physical posture of a speaker is a matter of personal preference, but you should follow a few general principles. Except for situations involving humor or other theatrical productions, speakers should have a professional appearance, one that's attentive and respectful of the audience. It's OK for a speaker to appear relaxed, but this should not extend to leaning on the podium or slouching.

Gestures and facial expressions should be vigorously used to bring a speaker's words to life. Expressive people who naturally use their hands while telling a story should do the same while giving a speech or presentation. You should also change your facial expressions to show feelings toward your words.

If you don't habitually use your hands expressively while talking, you should work on making gestures during a speech. Introverted speakers can start by adding a few gestures, perhaps with directional phrases ("the facility moved way out west" while sweeping an arm out to indicate direction), or phrases with size ("caught a very small fish," demonstrating by holding up your hand, showing your thumb close to your forefinger). Remember, it's easy and appears natural for most speakers to tick off three points on their fingers.

Since a presentation is typically given in front of a larger audience, and the speaker may be a bit constricted by standing behind a lectern, it's usually necessary for speakers to make their gestures more energetic. We've given many presentation training classes. We videotape student presentations, asking them to make their gestures more dramatic. We encourage them to really "push it out" during their talk. When our students watch the video, they are surprised to see the gestures that felt overdone look just about right at the lectern.

Eye gaze is important. It's not hard to control your eye movement during a presentation. It's a technique, however, often neglected due to the distractions of reading text, using audiovisual aids, and the pressure of being onstage. Looking at members of the audience immediately shows them the speaker is attentive to them. Once they see this, audience members think it's polite to devote their attention in return to the speaker. Depending on the physical layout of the site, most speakers will need to move and change eye gaze direction in an organized way to engage the audience in all areas of the room.

It's not necessary for the speaker to look directly into the eyes of individual members of the audience. Looking at a particular area of the room will have a halo effect of making a dozen people in that area believe they are the ones singled out by the speaker.

It's important to not change your eye gaze so quickly that you appear shifty-eyed. If a speaker's eye gaze only lingers in an area for a second or two at a time before moving rapidly away, the audience will get the impression of insincerity. Sustain your eye gaze to a particular area for 20 seconds or more before moving on to another area of the room.

Stage Kinetics

Stage kinetics—the speaker's movement around the room—also has visual impact. In the performing arts, this is a subject of careful study. Actors, dancers, and singers all move around the stage with purpose. Performers comfortable with the stage—such as comedians and motivational speakers—also use movement to add theatrical flair, change the mood of a discussion, and highlight changed emotion in their voice. Done well, the movement adds to the performance. The risk is that the movement will seem artificial, look awkward, and serve as a distraction.

Some managers recoil at the thought of moving around the stage; they fear coming out from behind the cover of the lectern. It's understandable to feel nervous about leaving the lectern's perceived comfort zone, but it offers a big payoff. Getting away from the lectern brings you closer to your audience.

In some oral presentation situations—like a Bible reading in a church service—it's most appropriate to stand behind a lectern. But for other speaking situations, we strongly advise you to create your own space, by standing to one side of the lectern. This will put you more in touch with your audience and will facilitate more natural hand and arm gestures.

Before you decide whether it's appropriate to move away from the lectern, you should consider the room's acoustics. If you're in a small room and no voice amplification is required, the problem is solved; the audience will hear you as well or better away from any lectern. If a system of microphones and speakers is in use, and the meeting has on-site audiovisual support, ask in advance for a wireless microphone.

This is a common request, and most audiovisual techs will have lavalier microphones for this purpose. Lavalier microphones clip onto a necktie, coat lapel, or shirt collar.

For most presenters, just standing next to the lectern, gesturing naturally, and using the other effective body language techniques will provide the audience with plenty of visual stimulation. But speakers can add dimension, reinforce a point, and add a sense of urgency by moving just a small distance.

In order to make a strong point, you can begin a statement, pause, and then take two or three purposeful steps forward, stop, and deliver the rest of your decisive line. Then, after speaking for a bit, you can retreat to your starting point.

In most cases, there's not much to be gained from further movement around the stage, and it's definitely a bad idea to wander aimlessly around the room while you speak. A few speakers like to walk completely around the room, like grade school teachers watching students for misbehavior; most experts agree this is distracting and unsettling to the audience.

One sin of stage kinetics is leaning from side to side, or rocking in place. Some speakers hope this swaying motion expresses dynamic feeling, but it does not. Audiences invariably comment negatively on the "rockers," saying such purposeless movement is distracting.

Paralinguistics

A number of nonverbal factors contribute to the way a speaker sounds, and include the tone, pitch, rhythm, volume, and inflection. With a little thought and planning, most speakers can vary these attributes. This makes a tremendous difference in bringing their words to life.

The easiest way to work out effective uses of these vocal techniques is by rehearsing your presentation. As you practice saying your lines aloud in varying tempos, changing the timing of pauses, tone, and inflections, you will discover many new ways to give your words meaning and impact.

Use of Humor

For a long time after World War II, from the 1950s to the mid-1990s, speakers started off their presentations with a joke or two, before getting into the serious substance of their speech. Professional speechwriters of the era needed a hefty joke file and a few fresh stories every week to keep up with the demand for humor.

Humor in public speaking is still alive and well, but the routine in which speakers told two full traditional jokes—with setups and punch lines—has become passé.

Today's effective speakers still recognize the value of humor as an icebreaker, putting the audience at ease, and establishing a friendly rapport. But instead of contrived jokes, they typically try to comment on something funny related to the subject matter or event.

Aside from the question of how to inject humor into your speech, ask yourself: Should you? There is a clear downside. What if no one laughs? Some experts, like well-known speaking coach Nick Morgan, say using humor is definitely not for everyone. "Humor is hazardous to the health of public speakers. You've got to do humor well or it falls flat— and that's worse than no humor at all" (Morgan, 2009).

Yet humor can make you likable, put the audience at ease, and bring your words to life in an entertaining way. Using humor can be risky, but if it is done in a way relatable to the audience or event, it's worth it.

For most speakers, the best way to add humor is to tell an anecdote or funny story about something that happened to them personally, or to someone around them. Humorous incidents from everyday life are easy to relate, and they come across as genuine. Self-effacing humor can be an especially powerful tool. It's easy, and effectively shows the audience you don't take yourself too seriously.

Edward J. Derwinski, who became the first Secretary of Veterans Affairs when the Veterans Administration was elevated to a Cabinet Department, had a signature technique in self-denigrating humor. During his frequent speeches to veterans organizations, he made sure his introduction included the fact that he had been a private in the army. Then, stepping to the lectern, Derwinski said he needed to correct the impression that he had not been able to gain superior rank during his service all through World War II: "Because of my instinctive leadership qualities, my command of military situations, and my ability to lead, when I left the army, I was a corporal." This always brought a big laugh, and warmed the audience toward him.

You should keep a joke file. But instead of outmoded jokes, fill your file with notes on amusing things that happen to you, cartoons that depict funny ways to look at your field of work, and other humorous contrasts from your observations and experience. This kind of humor may not get the audience rolling on the floor laughing, but it may provide the right touch to bring your words to life in a comfortable way.

Stage Fright

Remember Speech 101? Some of you will never forget the symptoms that built as you waited to give your talk in front of the class: your hands would sweat, your mouth would go dry, your knees trembled, and there was an uncontrollable blush spreading over your neck and face. You wanted to control those things, but they were a low priority compared with worries about your racing heart rate and butterflies in your stomach.

Fear hung in the air like diesel fumes as you approached the lectern. You looked to your fellow students for reassurance, but you didn't get much eye contact from others in speech class. Your classmates who were going to speak after you were busy rehearsing their lines in silent fear; those who had finished were slumped down, too relieved their ordeal was over to care.

Performance anxiety is a well-documented phobia, fueled by powerful chemical reactions in the body. Fear of speaking in public triggers the release of a substantial dose of adrenaline into the bloodstream, and the symptoms—reflecting the body's preparation for human fight-or-flight behavior—naturally follow.

Contrary to the way many speakers feel, people don't die from stage fright. Even if some speakers have serious heart issues, they don't die from being on stage. Stage fright won't kill you, but it might kill your chances of giving a good presentation. There are ways to reduce this huge, fearful situation to a more manageable size. First, consider who's affected by it and why, and then identify ways to counteract it.

Speech coaches like to point out that a majority of people list public speaking among their greatest fears—ahead of insects, heights, flying, and even death. It's fun for experts to say: "It appears people really mean it when they say they'd rather die than give a speech."

So stage fright is universal. Fear of speaking in public is not an individual affliction. It's a normal feeling, common to everyone who steps up to the lectern. Even professional entertainers feel the effects of this natural process—some quite strongly. But because they recognize the symptoms for what they are, the pros press on, using these feelings to stimulate more energy in their performance.

To confront stage fright, ask: "What am I afraid of?" It could be failure, rejection, looking foolish, or fear of the unknown. None of these are trivial matters or impossible outcomes. A speaker could definitely look foolish. But with proper preparation and a reasonable appraisal of the situation, you can be confident those fears will not be realized, and your presentation will result in a good experience. Stage fright is initially invisible to the audience. While you may feel your fear is obvious, the audience is not reading the symptoms. At least, the audience doesn't see the nervousness, unless the speaker announces the affliction, either in his own words, or by exhibiting one or more "stage fright giveaways."

A speaker might say, "I guess you can tell I'm a bit nervous," hoping to win either acceptance or sympathy from the audience. Unfortunately, this has the opposite effect, and causes discomfort among the audience as they then focus on the slightest mannerisms, looking for telltale signs of weakness. Nonverbal giveaways include holding onto the sides of the lectern in a rigid grip, jingling change in your pocket, wringing your hands together, and rapidly shifting your weight from foot to foot. Knowledgeable speakers can avoid these telltale signs, and not look like they have stage fright. But is it possible for them not to *feel* like they have it?

Rehearsal—The Fine-Tune Phase

It's a great idea to practice your talk with a stopwatch. Once you see how the timing works, you will need to edit your material to make the talk fit the allotted time, speaking at your normal pace. As you see how long it takes to give your presentation, make timing marks in your notes, highlighted in color. These navigation marks can include the half-way mark, a minute to go, and any other signals to yourself that might add to your comfort level.

When you actually give the speech, you'll probably find your pace varies a bit from your rehearsal. But the practice should get you very close to the actual timing. If you can rehearse in front of a captive audience such as friends and family, you'll make your practice timing even more accurate. While rehearsing, indulge your natural inclination to emphasize points with gestures, facial expressions, and changes in vocal inflection. If you plan to use props or references while on the stage, practice moving them into place in a smooth fashion. If you're planning to use audiovisuals that will require slide changes, practice using a remote without feeling constricted by it. Either put it down on the lectern, or hold it in an unobtrusive manner.

Put It All Together—The Speech

It's time to give your presentation. Walk up to the lectern, place your notes on top, and pause to look at the audience. Unless this is a very somber occasion—a eulogy—you should smile. The pause has a powerful effect of establishing your command of the situation. It will also calm your nerves. Don't bail out by giving a salutation or making a comment on the previous speaker. Use the compelling opening you've written, starting with your memorized first line.

As you develop your theme, move away from the lectern; stand next to it or within a couple feet. Remember to work the whole room with your eye gaze, and take the opportunities— which you discovered while rehearsing—to gesture naturally. Be enthusiastic as you warm to your subject, and use the facial expressions and changes in the vocal tone you anticipated earlier.

Keep track of time, making use of the marks you put in your notes during rehearsal. If you can, have a co-worker signal you from the back of the room when the time allotted your presentation is almost done. As you wind up your talk using that nice concluding line you wrote, stand silent for a few seconds at the lectern before walking away. It will be your time to enjoy the recognition of the audience for a great presentation!

Break This Rule: Practice in Front of a Mirror

By Karen Hough

Practicing in front of a mirror sounds like great advice. We don't know what we look like, and it's not always possible to videotape our practice, so why not? This rule is one of those that everybody knows is "right."

> *To give yourself the best possible chance of playing to your potential, you must prepare for every eventuality. That means practice.*
>
> **—Seve Ballesteros**

I've heard or read this tip countless times, and here's what happens when you practice in front of a mirror: You get used to performing for an "audience" that's about twelve inches away. You become obsessed with how you hold your face, the arc of your arm, and that part of your body you don't like. You think about yourself and how you look. You worry about tics you didn't notice before, or conversely, you really enjoy smiling back at that good-looking person in the mirror. In short, you practice watching yourself.

You're supposed to be practicing watching the audience! You won't be watching yourself when you present, but your body, voice, and energy will all be used to a mirror, which gives no feedback, reaction, or energy and makes you focus on yourself. Nothing will make you self-conscious and inwardly focused more quickly than practicing in front of a mirror.

There's a Greek legend about a hunter named Narcissus, who was renowned for his beauty. He was quite proud, so Nemesis decided to act. Nemesis was the goddess of retribution against those who succumbed to hubris, or overarching pride. She lured Narcissus to a pool where he saw his reflection. He fell in love with his own beauty and eventually wasted away and died, staring at his own reflection. Psychology has an illness named for the hunter—narcissism.

Merriam-Webster's dictionary defines narcissism as "egoism, egocentrism," and synonyms include self-absorption and self-centeredness. Of course, most people aren't remotely narcissists, but a mirror can make anyone worry too much about themselves. Too much self-reflection removes your focus from the audience. You just keep coming back to the reflection, rather than to reality. If we're centered on ourselves, instead of on our audiences, we'll kill a good presentation.

To feel the difference between a mirror and an open room, put your hand up in front of your face as though it's a mirror. Notice how it's several inches away, blocks your view of anything else, and makes the area around you feel small. When you practice in that "space," you keep your energy close and don't project your voice. Now stand at the front of an open room and look around. You can see all the way to the back wall. You realize that your energy and voice need to project to the front, sides, and rear of the room. You begin to notice details about the room and how you feel standing at the front.

This is the best way to practice presentations—in an open room, your hotel room, or a conference room. Get used to how your body feels and your voice sounds. Stumble through, mess up—so what. It's practice. And do it with an audience if you can swing it. Your best friend, spouse, or colleague will give you better feedback than any mirror ever will. You'll feel what it's like to have another person react to you, and you'll understand how energy and eye contact affect them.

Sure, practicing in front of a mirror, maybe once, might help you become aware of how you look. That's not an awful thing, but you've got to step away and feel the excitement and fear of facing a room. You may not look perfect, and that's just fine.

The whole world's a stage and most of us are desperately unrehearsed.

—Seán O'Casey

Real, on-your-feet preparation—there's no substitute. I had a man come up to me after a workshop laughing ruefully. "I was hoping your workshop would give me an out. I was looking for the magic pill; how I can be fabulous without practice. You just verified that there are no shortcuts."

Sorry, kids. Even when you're breaking all the rules, you've got to practice your badness! And I promise it's worth it. There's a staggering trend I've been tracking. My study isn't scientific, and I've not formally recorded the numbers, but at workshop after workshop, the people in the most senior positions are always the most prepared. They set aside time to organize, practice speeches out loud, or simply work through the purpose for their next meeting. This makes it pretty obvious how they got to that top job, doesn't it? These people tell me stories about their solid preparation habits even when they weren't at a senior level. People who are less experienced or lower in the org chart rush around making sure we know how busy they are—and wing it, wing it, wing it. Yep, the people who most need to prepare are the least likely to do so.

Figure 14-1 Mirrors are just a one-person show. Practice often, out loud, and on your feet!

I mean, come on. Do you really think Olympic athletes wing it?

Author Malcolm Gladwell studied people at the top of their fields. He found that it wasn't innate talent or intelligence that sent people to the top of their professions. It was practice and experience. He contends that it takes about ten thousand hours of real-time practice to catapult someone to the highest level of capabilities—whether as a computer programmer, concert pianist, athlete, or member of a rock 'n' roll band. The people who put in the time, work, and practice are the ones who excel. The Beatles, for example, played marathon eight-hour sets at strip clubs in advance of their celebrity. They had performed more than twelve hundred times before their first burst of fame in 1964.

That magic number—ten thousand hours—continues to pop up as the differentiator between people who work hard and do well, and those who work really, really hard and do incredibly well. Or in our case, are super bad.

So, what about natural talent? Believe it or not, there's more danger here for those who are naturally comfortable presenters, and less for those who are nervous and uncertain. People who know they need practice might at least feel guilty when they don't prepare. But I have a special warning for those who often receive praise and feel they can pull off a pretty good presentation without preparation. Your advantage is that you have tricks and natural grace that allow you to wing it. Your disadvantage is that you believe that's all you need. And the more you get used to winging it, the less time you'll devote to improvement. That's a mistake. Tony Schwartz, who has aggregated studies on this topic, says this:

> If you're not actively working to get better at what you do, there's a good chance you're getting worse, no matter what the quality of your initial training—in some cases, diminished performance is simply the result of a failure to keep up with the advances in a given field. But it's also because most of us tend to become fixed in our habits and practices, even when they're suboptimal.

I once had a member of my ensemble who was magnetic and smart but never prepared until the day of an event. Under pressure, it was clear that he hadn't looked up any new material and had not prepared very much. He could always come off as good and charming, but pretty soon I knew his entire bag of tricks and was onto his style. He lacked depth. I knew I'd never be able to send him to a client more than twice—they too would grow weary of his same old delivery. Buh-bye.

What we're talking about here is a plateau. When you reach a certain level of competence, your body and mind realize that it's good enough to get by on. And let's be honest—society rewards a certain level of competence and often doesn't expect more. The author Joshua Foer calls this concept the "OK Plateau." You're okay at something, you're competent, but despite months, even years, of practice, you do not improve. Foer's examples include typing—once we are able to type at a certain acceptable speed, we might remain at that speed for the rest of our lives despite hours of time spent typing. We can discover why with a deeper look at practice.

It's not necessarily the hours and hours you spend typing that allow you to improve. Truly improving requires conscious effort: trying more difficult techniques, pushing to increase your speed, and being willing to fail. The researchers K. Anders Ericsson, Ralf Krampe, and Clemens Tesch-Romer studied this phenomenon and called it "deliberate practice." Practice and experience are absolutely necessary to becoming a better typist, a better athlete, a better presenter. The more you do, the more situations and surprises you encounter, the better you become. However, only those who continually stretch, experiment, and fail will move toward expertise.

The Beatles were great by 1964 because of the inordinate amount of performing hours they had put in. But the second key here is that they had to keep getting better and playing new material. They had to cover hundreds of songs by dozens of bands and keep writing original songs. Otherwise, audiences would become bored with their set, and the club owners wouldn't hire them anymore. In the process of rehearsing, performing, and learning more complicated music, you can bet that The Beatles failed more times than they would ever admit. Every failure prodded them toward true expertise.

If I don't practice the way I should, then I won't play the way that I know I can.

—Ivan Lendl

Most people don't know that improvisers are the most over-rehearsed people in the performance industry. Surprised? You may think improvisers are just quick on their feet and throw it all together. But the truth is that improv troupes rehearse more than twice as much as casts for Shakespeare plays. They have to—there's no script, and no two performances are alike. Improv is an art form that happens in the moment without a script, props, or a plan, so improvisers spend exorbitant amounts of time practicing every possible scenario on stage. That's why, when you see a great improv show, it looks effortless. The key is that during practice, the troupe is always trying to surprise each other—coming up with the weirdest, most difficult audience suggestions imaginable. (And believe me, even the broadest imagination sometimes falls short of what an audience member will shout out.)

You know where I'm going with this. You've got to practice. Out loud, often, and on your feet. If you're one of the lucky people who has natural ability, understand that you're the most likely to become stagnant. If you're terrified, nervous, and inexperienced, you have nowhere to go but up. Practice will make an astonishing difference in your ability to be effective, influential, and wow your audience. Most of the problems I first see when people present can usually be ironed out with two or three run-throughs. Do any of these sound familiar?

- **Running long or out of time**—Reading through your speech silently or whispering it to yourself will never approximate the true amount of time it will take to say it out loud and on your feet. And the more you practice, the more you will become aware of time. We often ask people to prepare a three-minute presentation, and they have no idea that their time is up when they've barely completed their intro. As you practice, your body will actually be able to feel how much time has passed because you'll become accustomed to how long it takes to get through certain amounts of material.

- **Stumbling over your words**—If you don't say them out loud, you won't realize that the brilliant phrases you've written or imagined are impossible to say. Lyricists know that even if they believe their words will fit a song perfectly, they never really know until someone tries to sing it.
- **Going up or going blank**—"Going up" is a theater term for when an actor forgets a major part of the script and skips ahead. That's always a scramble because then the other actors have to figure out a way to justify what's happening! "Going blank" is, of course, entirely forgetting what you're supposed to say. One of the most common reasons for going blank is that you've never given your body, voice, and mind the experience of standing in front of an open room, sea of faces, or group of chairs. You get messed up by the acoustics of the room, the distraction of the people in it, or simply the sensation of trying to hold yourself in a standing position.

Improvisation works only after an enormous amount of thought and practice.

—Rafael Viñoly

So do it! Start practicing and get used to stumble-throughs. People often want to bail out when their first run-through is rough. But that's the point. It should be ragged, difficult, and full of mistakes. Then you figure out what to change. The next time is a little better, and the next even better. Why would you want to submit your audience, and that critical speech, to your first unpleasant dry run? In her book *Bird by Bird*, Anne Lamott makes a wonderful point about writing that applies here. She notes that all good writers write terrible first drafts. So, if a rotten first draft, or an awful first run-through, is part of the process, why not embrace it?

Many of us deal with a lot of fear when we're faced with presenting to a crowd. That's natural. Practice will help manage that fear. I'm not going to promise that it will ever go away completely, but it's a part of you, and the more you get back on that horse, the better rider you'll become.

Practice isn't the thing you do once you're good. It's the thing you do that makes you good.

—Malcolm Gladwell

My favorite piece of bad advice is that you present in every low-risk venue you can scare up. It's better to experiment in a place where you don't have so much at stake. Groups everywhere would love to hear you speak: your local youth club on baking a holiday cake, your place of worship on managing finances, your book club on meeting an author. There are tons of places where you can try out a new hook or practice moving around the stage. That way, you'll have places to fail, get up, try again, and figure out what works for you. Then when it is time to give a critical speech to a committee at work, you'll be confident and ready.

And heck yeah, I know you're busy! And I know you really want to skip this part because you only present once per quarter. But if you start baking practice into your schedule, even a little bit, you'll be a badder you. Book time on your calendar, leave your home or office, or promise your friends cookies if they'll watch you for thirty minutes. Whatever it takes. When the presentation is down pat, you can handle all the little unexpected things that might come up and just be yourself—rather than going blank because you didn't practice. This is about *doing*.

The Six Final Insights to Master

Jeanette Henderson and Roy Henderson

On Site Before the Event

Luck is when preparation meets opportunity.

—Anonymous

As the Presenter, you should try, whenever possible, to arrive at the venue before the audience does, in order to take the opportunity to become familiar with the room. Upon your arrival, you should, walk around the room, getting a feel for its size and acoustics as discussed earlier.

You should stand behind the lectern, make sure that it is the right height, and see whether it is adjustable. If someone before you changes that height, you'll want to know how to change it back. If it's not the right height, change it now while you have the chance. If it turns out to be the wrong height for someone else, let him change it. If he didn't bother to learn how, too bad; he should have come in and checked it as you did.

Check out the lighting and sound if possible, both on the lectern and in the room. Check that the reading light on the lectern, if there is one, is functioning properly, and decide whether you're going to need

Jeanette Henderson and Roy Henderson, "The Six Final Insights to Master," There's No Such Thing as Public Speaking: Make Any Presentation or Speech as Persuasive as a One-on-One Conversation, pp. 190-208, 212-216. Copyright © 2007 by Penguin Group USA. Reprinted with permission.

it. If possible, check that any spotlights to be used are properly aligned; this will prevent a direct blinding light or a reflecting glare, which might interfere when you read your script or notes.

You should check the microphone to see if it can be moved (truly, there's nothing worse than watching someone try to move an immovable mike), and to ensure that it points at the correct angle upward toward the second button down on your dress shirt or the equivalent. You should check the sound level by having a helper stand at the back to confirm that you can be heard, taking into consideration that there will more noise when the room is filled with people.

Naturally, you should report any problems immediately to the person coordinating the event, and check them again immediately upon adjustment. Honestly, a good technical staff will appreciate a Presenter who knows what he needs, and will generally do everything possible to accommodate you, as that is their job. Their frustration comes in when the Presenter doesn't know what to ask for, then complains later because something isn't right.

Even when no professional technical staff is present, it is a safe bet that *somebody*, somewhere in the host group, has been given responsibility for providing adequate technical support, and they, too, will welcome the chance to satisfy your needs.

Once you have assured yourself that your technical needs have been met, you should take a moment to select approximately where your focal points will be, and walk the path you will be expected to walk when you are introduced. You should take note of any steps, ledges, wires, or curtains that must be navigated, so that no unexpected trips or falls (a Presenter's worst nightmare) occur during your entrance or approach to the lectern.

Finally, you should spend a few moments behind the lectern, with or without speaking, and get as comfortable with that space as if you were in your own office, behind your own desk. This is your workspace for this event, and it should feel as familiar as possible.

Naturally, all of this preparation can occur only if you arrive early enough to perform these tasks without an audience. We highly recommend that you—particularly if you are a less-experienced

Presenter—arrive sufficiently early to carry out this procedure, even when it means you will have time to kill before your presentation. You might even consider doing your walk-through, then leaving and coming back again later for the presentation. There can seldom be too many precautions or too much preparation.

Should an audience already be present by the time you arrive, you will simply have to make these mental observations as best you can prior to the beginning of your presentation, though this leaves much more to chance. Nevertheless, knowing what to look for as you wait to make your presentation can do much to preserve your integrity and confidence.

As the Event Begins

Nature has given men one tongue, but two ears, that we may hear from others twice as much as we speak.

—Epictetus

Obviously, what occurs between the time of your arrival to the time of your presentation will vary depending on the situation. In some cases, you may be obliged to socialize with your hosts; however, as a general rule, you should remain isolated from your Reactors for as long as possible prior to the beginning of the event.

As every professional performer knows, making an entrance can be a very valuable tool, creating quite desirable anticipation within the Reactor. Provided this anticipation is used properly (rather than abused, such as arriving much later than expected), it can prove to be quite useful in establishing the right kind of authoritative image.

In general, there are two distinct types of public events: those where the Presenter remains in view prior to his presentation, such as dinner speeches and panel discussions, and those where the Presenter remains off-stage or in another room until he has been introduced, at which time he moves to the lectern and stands alone on the podium. Since the events that occur *after* arriving at the lectern are the same, let's take a look at what needs to occur before that time.

When the Speaker Remains in View

When you must remain in view of the audience during your introduction or others' presentations, it is extremely important that you give your full attention to every other Presenter who speaks before you. This may sound obvious, yet when you take notice of how poorly many people behave toward a speaker as they sit at a head table, you'll see this is a necessary reminder.

When you pay attention to those who speak before you, it serves several purposes. First, it demonstrates that you are a courteous person—a universally desirable trait, especially in a potential ally to the Reactor. When you fail to pay attention, when you let yourself be distracted by your surroundings, your dinner, your friends in the crowd, or your own notes or script, your movements will pull focus from the current Presenter. Reactors will find themselves looking at you, wondering what you are doing, rather than listening to what that other Presenter is saying.

It is extremely discourteous to appear to ignore other Presenters. It telegraphs to the Reactor that you don't feel the other Presenters are important. When a Reactor sees you ignoring another Presenter, your apparent lack of respect will come across loud and clear. When you set a precedent that it is acceptable to ignore other Presenters, chances are *you* will be ignored when your turn arrives.

When you do pay attention to the current Presenter, you are telegraphing to the Reactor that what that Presenter is saying is important, and should be listened to. When she sees you paying attention, she, too, will pay attention. You have, in fact, put in a Cause to create leadership (you looked), and she follows you by reacting with Effect (she looks). She is already behaving as your Reactor, and you haven't even said a word!

At the same time, you have also indicated to your Reactor that you are alike, that you are both Reactors at this moment in time, that you are both experiencing the same thing, that you are connected by this mutual event. In other words, you are already accomplishing the first step in your Formula for Inspiration, by identifying with your Reactor, again, without saying a word.

When you are part of a team of Presenters making a unified presentation, this becomes even more important. A Presenter who fails to listen to someone on his *own* team will diminish the authority of himself, the entire team, and the team's message as well.

Finally, by paying close attention to the previous Presenters, becoming a Reactor yourself for that moment in time, you focus your mind on something besides your own upcoming speech. This waiting period can sometimes be a bit destructive, particularly for less experienced Presenters, allowing nerves to pile up and up. Provided you are sufficiently prepared, it is much more constructive to use this time to open the doors toward identifying with your Reactor than to be worried about what will come soon enough.

The Introduction

The hardest part of a lecture is waking up the audience after the man who introduces me has concluded his remarks.

—Anonymous

First and foremost, whenever possible, you should arrange to have someone introduce you. By doing so, you automatically create authority. The Reactor will see that you are important enough to *have* someone introduce you, which has a credibility factor all its own, and will respond with suitable respect for your position.

In addition, you should provide the introduction, or at least the information you wish to be included in the introduction. This will save you from having to say anything about yourself at the beginning of your presentation, which is generally very bad form. You can also tailor the introduction to suit the particular group of Reactors and/or that particular presentation.

Let's see what normally happens during an introduction. While the Introducer is extolling the Presenter's virtues, the Reactor, at some point, will be compelled to turn her attention from that Introducer to you, the Presenter-in-waiting. This is such a strong tendency that even during televised presentations, the camera will almost always get a view of the person being introduced at some point during that introduction.

The impression made at that moment is an incredibly lasting one, so that moment must be everything it can be. Unfortunately, more often than not, that moment is wasted and often sets a bad tone for the rest of the presentation.

For example, should the Reactor find that the Presenter-in-waiting is looking someplace other than toward the Introducer—such as at other people or distractions in the back of the room, at his plate, his fingernails, or his notebook—the Reactor will start to wonder what it is the Presenter *is* looking at. In fact, the Reactor may be so intent to find out what is so fascinating to the Presenter that she will become distracted from what the Introducer is saying about him, and she will hear none of the introduction. If she doesn't hear the introduction, which is designed to demonstrate the Presenter's authority and credibility, then he has lost an opportunity to establish one of the most fundamental necessities of his presentation.

Whenever a Presenter fails to pay attention to the Introducer, the Reactor will likely interpret his inattentiveness as an indication that the introduction lacks importance. When a Presenter decides something isn't important enough to listen to, the Reactor gets that message loud and clear, and responds in kind. After all, if he, her potential leader, doesn't think the information is important enough to pay attention to, why should she? Again, if she doesn't hear the introduction, he's lost ground.

Just as with previous Presenters, you must focus on your Introducer with rapt attention, in order to telegraph to your Reactor that what the Introducer is saying is important. Your attention must be unwavering throughout the entire introduction, with one momentary exception: a quick nod of acknowledgment at the appropriate moment. As mentioned earlier, at some point during the introduction, the audience will be compelled to look at you. When you sense that happening (and you will if you are attuned and waiting for it), it is perfectly acceptable and highly recommended that you briefly turn to your audience and give a short nod of acknowledgment. This will meet the minimum standards of the norm of that situation. Once you have completed the nod, you should immediately return your focus to the Introducer.

This again will telegraph to the Reactor that while you have invited her into the conversation with an acknowledgment, it will also remind her that the Introducer is, for that moment in time, the one requiring our attention. She will quickly follow your look and return her attention to the Introducer.

Obviously, this situation only applies when you are in view of your Reactors prior to your presentation, and particularly during the introduction. When you are coming out from backstage or another room, you need only be concerned with getting to the lectern. Before we discuss that, however, we have to deal with the reality that most Presenters will be feeling at this point: a case of the butterflies.

The Adrenaline Factor

It should be evident that when you have everything we've just discussed to think about and to do while waiting for your presentation to begin, you will have much less time to get nervous about it. The nervousness felt by a Presenter prior to his presentation, however, is both expected and absolutely essential. In fact, it can be one of the more useful tools at your disposal, provided you handle it properly.

It is useless to try to get rid of that nervous energy because frankly, that's nearly impossible for all except the most experienced or hardened Presenters. Rather than ignore it, and risk having that adrenaline overwhelm your good senses, it is better to learn to channel it into something productive.

By recognizing that this rush of adrenaline is inevitable, you will also realize that *where* the adrenaline goes is controlled only by where you choose to send it. Just as we can use it to miraculously flip over cars in a crisis, we can direct it wherever we want it to go, as long as we decide ahead of time where that will be.

The natural tendency is for that adrenaline to go where your body thinks it is needed at the moment it is released, and it will usually first present itself in the movements you make on your way to the lectern. Very often a Presenter will literally bound out of his chair or from backstage, then race to the lectern as fast as possible, hopefully not tripping over his own feet or other obstacles along the way.

Usually that leap is followed by the Presenter grabbing the lectern to try to stop his forward motion, or to calm himself. Once he grabs hold of the lectern, of course, all of the other destructive, contortionist things already mentioned will start to occur.

Chances are the race to the lectern did little to quell the adrenaline anyway, so the next place it manifests itself is in the speaking mechanism. Out of control, the Presenter usually starts talking as fast as he can. Often that talking begins while he's wrestling the microphone into place, and continues as he pulls out his notes. Mostly it's gibberish until he gets himself set, further confirming his lack of preparation. All the while, he's probably frantically trying to catch eye contact with as many people as possible, which, of course, creates the dreaded shifty-eyed look right off the bat.

Even after the Presenter has his microphone and notes in place, that adrenaline is still likely circulating, looking for somewhere else to be expended. That usually translates into very rapid speaking at the beginning of the presentation, exactly the opposite of what we need at this point. Remember, we want our Reactor to settle into the, sound of our voice, so we must speak even more slowly at the beginning than we normally would.

Eventually, after several minutes or more, the Presenter might finally recover from his frenetic moments, his adrenaline will finally settle down, and he might start to make some sense. A great deal of time and energy has been wasted, however, and it will be a struggle for him to gain (or rather, regain) his authority, which has predictably suffered from a weak opening.

get the Effect of getting her to look back to the current Presenter, thus making her an instant follower of yours.

This takes us up to the time of your introduction. Again, you are paying full attention to your Introducer, and so is your Reactor. At one point during the introduction it will be appropriate for you to turn and nod to your Reactor, but then you must return your full attention to the Introducer.

Now the moment has come. Your introduction is complete and it is time for you to move toward the lectern. When rising from a seated position, whether you are at the head table or somewhere nearby, you should stand, move behind your seat, and push your seat back under the table. This demonstrates to the Reactor that you are deliberate, organized, and even tidy, strengthening that sense of authority by exhibiting qualities most Reactors will admire in a leader.

Usually when seated, a man or woman wearing a jacket will have it unbuttoned for comfort. Now that you are standing, you should button your jacket. This will put you in a one-step-up position in attire, as everyone still seated has his or her jacket unbuttoned. The buttoning action will probably be blocked from view by the chair, providing you stay there until the task is accomplished.

Once your jacket is buttoned, or you have otherwise straightened out your attire as needed, you should pick up your notebook and *take a deep, calming breath*. This will create a very useful pause, which will accomplish several very positive things. First, it gives you time to visualize your adrenaline bubble and start it on its path to your feet, and to get your feet in the right place before moving forward, a precaution against a possibly embarrassing trip or stumble. Most stumbles occur on the first step or two, due to the Presenter being in an unbalanced position because he tries to move too quickly, usually because of the excess energy.

The deep breath, of course, will also assist in grounding any butterflies you may be experiencing, and buys you another moment to stand up straight and further collect yourself.

Now, you must begin to walk slowly and deliberately to the lectern, looking only at the person who has introduced you, or at the lectern should there be no other person on stage. This is the beginning of letting your Reactor have the opportunity to begin fully "checking you out," so you should never look at the audience as you make your way to the lectern!

Should you look at your Reactor while you are walking to the lectern, you rob her of the opportunity to satisfy that initial visual curiosity, as she will still be afraid of getting caught if you should catch her eye. Therefore, *you should never look toward your Reactor until she has had sufficient time to fully satisfy that curiosity.* This will take only a few moments once the attention has been called to you. Failure to allow her that time now will force her to take that look later—and that will distract her from listening.

...

When Murphy's Law Prevails

Everything that can go wrong will.

—**Murphy's Law**

You now know exactly what to do to prepare for your presentation, from the content of your message to the layout of your notes or script. You know how to use focuses, even when the room is too large to make eye contact, by using surrogates. You know what you must do with your body language, your voice, and your attire, and how to make the most of the technical tools you have at your disposal. You know that you must simply have a conversation with one person at a time, with a lot of other people eavesdropping.

You are fully prepared to deal with all of the things that normally happen during a presentation, and you should feel more comfortable than you ever thought possible under such circumstances. You are in complete control of everything with which you can be in control. But what happens when something unexpected and out of your control goes wrong?

Of course, there will always be the chance that certain uncontrollable events may occur during your presentation. Regardless of what happens, how you handle these momentary crises will make the most lasting impression of your presentation. When you play your cards right, however, you can also make the most positive impression possible. So when Murphy's Law does prevail, it is essential for you to know how to handle the proverbial worst-case scenario in order to come out smelling like a rose.

In the event of almost any technical malfunction, such as when the microphone stops working, the lights go out, or some other audio or visual difficulty occurs, it is essential you appear to remain *in control*. Maintaining authority is the most effective way to ensure that the level of respect for you remains as high as possible.

Everyone, both Presenter and Reactor, accepts the reality that occasionally, technical difficulties will occur. When they do, there are only three possible outcomes: (1) the Presenter will take complete control of the situation, (2) the Presenter will completely lose control of the situation, or (3) the Presenter merely abdicates control of the situation. The only desirable outcome is the first. Unfortunately, the most natural reaction usually results in one of the last two.

Face the Facts

The most common old wives' tale guiding the Presenter's reaction to technical difficulties is to continue on as though nothing has happened. While this may be expected during a performance of a die-hard theatrical group (which is working in a make-believe world anyway, so the situation can be anything they want it to be, including dark and silent), it is entirely unsuitable for a speaking engagement.

Let's face it: When a Presenter continues unabated through obvious technical problems such as a blackout, he will appear to be utterly disconnected with reality. Such a disconnect will make him look like an idiot. When a Reactor sees a Presenter ignoring the obvious, what in the world is she supposed to expect from him in an Alliance?

Stay in Control

Just as detrimental is when the Presenter stops and points out whatever it is that has gone wrong ("Gee, the lights went out!") as though someone needed to be told! This is usually followed by a request or demand that something be done immediately. When a Presenter has to ask for help, it diminishes his authority, which makes him appear out of control.

Worst of all, the Presenter will try to do something to fix the situation himself. This is a disastrous move, since it means that the Presenter must drop his role of authority and reclaim the role of technician. Since the chances are that he will be unable to fix the problem, he will have demonstrated that he couldn't live up to that lesser role, leaving huge doubt that he is able to live up to his greater role. When a *real* technician comes along to fix it, the humiliation will be complete. No chance of a meaningful connection with the audience after that!

In every case, the Presenter and his message are completely under mined by things that are obviously out of his control. He has been unable to demonstrate his ability to take control, therefore his ability to lead is understandably called into question.

Make Lemonade

Of course, that leaves just one easy and very deliberate way to overcome technical difficulties while maintaining absolute control: Do nothing. As Presenter, you should stop everything you are doing. You should say nothing, except possibly, to your Reactor, a simple, "One moment please." You should then gaze meaningfully, though never angrily or accusingly or frantically, at whoever is in charge of the technical aspects of the event, or the host, should the technical person be out of sight. Then wait.

It should come as little surprise that such a technician, who will suddenly feel an enormous amount of pressure for obvious reasons, will move extremely quickly to the source of the problem. No doubt the technician (or whoever is serving in that capacity) will very hurriedly issue a status report, and will give an estimate of how soon the problem will be resolved.

Without saying a word of explanation, without blaming anyone, without becoming a technician yourself, without having to make any apology, and without skipping a beat, you have succeeded in maintaining every element of control. So much action was accomplished on your behalf, without you having to say a word, that the Reactor is compelled to see you as a person who really gets things done. This is exactly the kind of person with whom she will want to have an Alliance, someone she can trust to get the job done, quickly, effectively, and with panache.

Once the problem is resolved, you need only say, "Thank you for your patience," and begin where you left off, or perhaps repeat the last thought byte prior to the mishap to enforce the last image the Reactor received from you.

You should never try to explain the problem, lest the images you create supersede and distract the Reactor from those already created from your message. Better to let your earlier images sink in further during this extra-long pause, rather than try to replace them with unimportant nonsense that fails to progress the plot.

You should also never try to place blame, nor do anything more than thank your Reactor for her patience. As we mentioned, we all recognize that these things happen, and it only makes sense to be understanding and realistic about it, and carry on as before as soon as possible.

There are few opportunities that hold so much potential danger yet can add such enormous strength to a Presenter's presentation when handled effectively. Once you demonstrate you can successfully overcome such an occurrence without batting an eye, it becomes very apparent to the Reactor that you could likely overcome anything. By virtue of a technical accident, you have made huge strides toward demonstrating that you are just the kind of person she can trust with her future. Your success as a Presenter and a leader are secured.

CPSIA information can be obtained
at www.ICGtesting.com
Printed in the USA
LVOW13s2058310517

536477LV00004B/6/P